TRADITIONAL

Irish

COOKING

———

On food, the great Dubliner,
John Swift, proclaimed:

Promises and pie-crust are made to be broken.

TRADITIONAL

Irish

COOKING

—

*The Fare of Old Ireland
and its History*

Andy Gravette and Debbie Cook

Garnet
PUBLISHING

TRADITIONAL IRISH COOKING
THE FARE OF OLD IRELAND AND ITS HISTORY

Published by
Garnet Publishing Ltd
8 Southern Court, South Street, Reading, RG1 4QS, UK

Copyright © Andy Gravette and Debbie Cook 2008

First Edition

ISBN 978-1-85964-155-2

British Library Cataloguing-in-Publication Data.
A catalogue record for this book is available from the British Library.

House editor Emma Hawker and Dan Nunn
Design by David Rose and Mike Hinks
Typeset by Samantha Barden
Front cover illustration by Janette Louden

Printed in Lebanon

CONTENTS

Fabulous Fare and a Rich Heritage

Almost everyone is familiar with Irish cream and butter and, of course, Ireland's famous stout and whiskey. However, much of the country's traditional fare is less well known, except perhaps by those who have been fortunate enough to visit the 'Emerald Isle'. Recently, Irish cookery has undergone something of a renaissance, as the restaurants and bistros of its two capitals, Dublin and Belfast, have gained reputations for presenting diners with superb modern dishes based on the best of Irish ingredients. The classic dishes of rural Ireland, however, remain the country's mainstay. Boxty and bannocks, colcannon and champ are just a few of the traditional dishes that contribute to the rich variety of this country's cuisine. These recipes, together with such delights as drisheen and dankey stew, reflect the culinary ingenuity of the Irish people, and are fundamentals of the Irish country kitchen. Irish food remains basically simple. It consists of local ingredients used at their best so that fresh, wholesome and succulent food can still be enjoyed now as it was thousands of years ago.

It is through the homely recipes of traditional Ireland that the rich tapestry of Irish history can be traced. For many millennia, Ireland has been an agricultural country, and fields on the island today were cultivated in pre-historic times. 'Time is the best storyteller' is an early Irish saying that can be applied equally to the country's food.

In this book we have combined snippets from Irish history with descriptions of various ingredients and typical traditional Irish recipes, demonstrating the link between the country's past and its present-day cuisine.

Using the Recipes

All the recipe ingredients are given in metric, imperial and American cup measures. Where the names are different, American terms are given in brackets.

All spoon measurements are level. You should use accurate measuring spoons for best results, using a 5 ml spoon for 1 teaspoon and a 15 ml spoon for 1 tablespoon.

Unless otherwise stated, the ingredients included in the recipes – such as vegetables or fruit – are medium size. All fresh ingredients should be washed and peeled where necessary.

Medium-sized eggs are used in all cases, except where stated otherwise. Eggs should always be eaten by the sell-by date and should never be used if the shells are already cracked. Pregnant women, the very young, the elderly and anyone with a specific medical condition should refer to approved guidelines before eating eggs and should particularly avoid raw or partially cooked eggs.

Fresh herbs are preferable to dried varieties. Dried herbs can be substituted where fresh herbs are unavailable, but half the quantity indicated is sufficient. Fresh herbs can easily be grown at home and they do impart a unique flavour to some of the recipes.

Can weights are approximate as they vary between brands.

Canned beans and pulses can be used instead of dried. If you substitute canned for dried, the weight of the prepared ingredients will be about twice the weight of the dried ingredients. For example, if the recipe calls for 225 g/ 8 oz/1⅓ cups dried pulses, substitute with a 425 g/15 oz/ large can. Note that dried kidney beans contain harmful toxins and should always be fast-boiled for around 20 minutes to destroy the toxins.

Some of the recipes contain whole or chopped nuts or nut oil and are therefore not suitable for young children or those with any form of nut-related allergy.

Oven settings vary considerably between different types of cooker, so you should check and adjust the cooking temperatures to suit your own oven. Gas ovens, for example, are hotter towards the top of the oven, while if you are using a fan-assisted oven, you may need to reduce the oven temperature.

Cooking times indicated in the recipes are approximate and are usually rounded up to the nearest five minutes. Fan ovens tend to cook faster than others so always refer to your handbook and adjust times to suit your own equipment.

Baking

From the grasses that grew wild in prehistoric times, a range of cereals developed – such as millet, sorghum, rice, maize, wheat, barley and oats – which came to be cultivated by early peoples. Our word 'cereal' comes from the Roman goddess of the harvest, Ceres, as it was the Romans who brought the use of grains to Britain and thence to Ireland, where many grew well in the temperate climate.

Many different cereals are ground to produce flour for baking or cooking, but only wheat produces a flour with rising properties, due to its high gluten content – gluten being the sticky, nitrogenous part of the flour which absorbs water. The more gluten in the flour, the better the rising qualities of the mix, so the strong, or brown, flours are the ones used in Irish yeast and bread baking. Softer flours, with a lower gluten content but a higher starch content, are reserved for making cakes and biscuits, as the starch ensures that the flour absorbs more fat, and a raising agent is added to the dough to compensate for the lower gluten.

Boxty on the griddle,
Boxty in the pan,
If you don't eat Boxty,
You'll never get a man.

———

Old Irish rhyme

All kinds of flour are used in the baking of Irish breads. If the whole of the wheat berry is ground, the flour is wholemeal or wholewheat, which is high in dietary fibre as it contains the bran, or outer husk. Often, however, the bran is removed after grinding. Some Irish breads used to use wheatmeal flour, which is flour with about ten per cent of the bran removed, although this type of flour is no longer readily available. Wheatgerm is the nutritious layer between the husk and the grain itself, and is often used in baking to add vitamins and minerals to the diet. Ordinary white flour is made from just the starch and gluten of the grain, with the bran and wheatgerm removed. Malted wheat flour has had malted wheat added to it to improve its flavour and texture, and is usually used in bread-making. Granary flour contains coarsely ground grain. Any type of flour can be ground between stones, in which case it is called stoneground.

In early times in Ireland, most grain was ground in water-driven mills, many of which still exist, such as the nineteenth-century example at Annalong in the Mourne mountains, where there were once 20 working mill wheels in the seventeenth and eighteenth centuries. One of the oldest surviving mills is located on the former grain-growing peninsula of Ards, at Ballycopeland in County Down. Built in the 1780s, it was a working mill until 1915 and has recently been reconstructed. The mill complex includes the miller's house, dust-house and kiln, where the grain is dried before milling. Three sets of mill wheels are still driven on a tributary of the River Clare, near Tuam in County Galway. They were constructed in the seventeenth century and now serve as the focal point of a corn-milling museum.

There were also a number of windmills built where running water was not available, but few have survived. Blennerville Windmill, near Tralee, was built in around 1800 and remained a working mill until 1880. The five-storey mill has now been renovated to show examples of mill operation from the nineteenth century. This is by no means the tallest existing windmill in Ireland, as the ruins of the mill near Dundalk stand seven storeys high. Tacumshane Windmill was built in 1846, near Wexford, and has also been restored. There is also an old windmill attached to the Guinness Museum in Dublin, known as St Patrick's Tower.

In the home, corn would be ground with a hand-operated millstone known as a quern. Traditionally, breads, muffins, biscuits and cakes, known locally as *kets*, were cooked on a griddle over the open fire. Breads cooked this way tend to keep longer than those baked in an oven. During the seventeenth century, however, many poorer people substituted potatoes for bread as their staple food, as corn was so expensive.

Today's baking delights are more imaginative than those of early times. Herb breads and rolls are lending a flavour of the countryside to the baker's tray. These are made by adding finely chopped fresh herbs and olive oil to the dough. Cheese and onion, and walnut with olive oil breads are also becoming popular in Irish cuisine.

Barley, now used in making Irish whiskey, was known to have been cultivated in Ireland as long ago as 3000 BC. The Greek writer Diocorides wrote that the Irish drank a brew made from malted barley known as *curmi*, flavoured with herbs. In the *Seanchus Mor*, a text written in 441 AD, it was recorded that barley was reserved solely for brewing purposes. The most famous of the Irish beers is, of course, stout, which is given its dark, distinctive colour by adding roasted barley to the brew of sieved, roasted and mashed barley and hops.

Oats are one of the earliest of grains to have been cultivated, and closely resemble the original grasses from which they developed. Highly nutritious – containing vitamin B, calcium, iron, protein, fats and carbohydrates – hulled oat grains are ground into fine, medium and coarse oatmeal, which is used extensively in traditional Gaelic cookery and is the basis of porridge. When the grains are passed through heated rollers, rolled oats are produced.

Rye is a hardy cereal rarely grown in Ireland and is more common in continental Europe, but it is sometimes used in Irish baking with wholemeal flour to prevent breads becoming stodgy and close-textured.

SERVES

4

CLASSIC BOXTY

225 g/8 oz potatoes, coarsely grated and dried

225 g/8 oz potatoes, boiled and mashed

2 eggs

1 small onion, finely grated

2 tablespoons plain (all-purpose) flour

3½ tablespoons milk

1 teaspoon salt

½ teaspoon freshly ground black pepper

50 g/2 oz/¼ cup butter

Beat together both types of potato and the eggs, then add all the remaining ingredients except the butter to make a firm mixture. Melt the butter in a large frying pan, then add 2–3 large spoonfuls of the mixture to the pan. Fry the boxties for 3 minutes on each side until golden brown and crisp. Serve immediately with grilled bacon or Apple Sauce (page 155).

FARMHOUSE FARLS

SERVES
4

'Farl' actually means quarter, so this bread is made in a circle and cut into four.

Sift all the ingredients except the oil and buttermilk into a bowl and make a well in the centre. Pour in the oil, then slowly add enough of the buttermilk to mix to a soft dough; you may not need to use it all. Turn out and knead for about 1 minute until smooth, then roll out on a lightly floured board into a thin, flat cake about 23 cm (9 inches) in diameter. Cut a deep cross in the cake, making four farls. Cook the farls for 8 minutes on each side on a moderately hot griddle or in a heavy-based frying pan but be careful not to let them burn. Slit the farls in half and serve with butter or cream and jam.

450 g/1 lb/4 cups plain
(all-purpose) flour
¾ teaspoon bicarbonate of soda
(baking soda)
¼ teaspoon salt
¼ teaspoon sugar
1 teaspoon corn oil
450 ml/¾ pint/2 cups buttermilk

TRADITIONAL SODA BREAD

MAKES
one 450 g/1 lb loaf

225 g/8 oz/2 cups wholemeal
(wholewheat) flour

300 g/10 oz/2½ cups plain
(all-purpose) flour

1 teaspoon bicarbonate of soda
(baking soda)

1 teaspoon salt

2 tablespoons unsalted (sweet)
butter

300 ml/½ pint/1¼ cups buttermilk

Many Irish breads are made with buttermilk, which you can buy in major supermarkets. If you do not have any, simply add a quarter of a teaspoon of lemon juice to ordinary milk.

Preheat the oven to 200°C/400°F/gas mark 6. Sift the wholemeal flour with 225 g/8 oz/2 cups of plain flour, then stir in the bran remaining in the sieve, the bicarbonate of soda and salt. Rub in the butter, then make a well in the centre. Pour in the buttermilk and stir together to make a crumbly dough. Dust a work surface with the remaining flour, turn out the dough and knead briefly until smooth and elastic. Shape into a round about 5 cm (2 inches) thick, dust with flour and cut a 2.5 cm (1 inch) deep cross in the top, almost dividing it into four quarters. Place on a greased baking sheet and bake in the oven for 35 minutes until hollow-sounding when tapped on the base. Cool on a wire rack.

COUNTRY WHITE SODA BREAD

———

Preheat the oven to 200°C/400°F/gas mark 6. Sift the dry ingredients into a bowl, then rub in the butter. Whisk the egg into the buttermilk, then stir into the dry ingredients and mix to a soft dough. Turn out on to a lightly floured board and knead for 1–2 minutes until smooth. Shape into a circle about 23 cm (9 inches) in diameter, flatten slightly and cut a deep cross in the centre, almost dividing it into four quarters. Place on a greased baking sheet and bake in the oven for 30–40 minutes until hollow-sounding when tapped on the base. Cool on a wire rack.

MAKES
one 450 g/1 lb loaf

450 g/1 lb/4 cups plain (all-purpose) flour

2 teaspoons cream of tartar

1 teaspoon bicarbonate of soda (baking soda)

¼ teaspoon salt

2 tablespoons butter, softened

1 egg

600 ml/1 pint/2½ cups buttermilk

SWEET IRISH SODA BREAD

MAKES
one 450 g/1 lb loaf

450 g/1 lb/4 cups plain (all-purpose) flour
1 teaspoon salt
½ teaspoon bicarbonate of soda (baking soda)
25 g/1 oz/2 tablespoons butter
100 g/4 oz/⅔ cup currants
1 teaspoon caster (superfine) sugar
300 ml/½ pint/1¼ cups buttermilk

If you don't have buttermilk, just add a quarter of a teaspoon of lemon juice to fresh milk.

Preheat the oven to 180°C/350°F/gas mark 4. Sift the flour, salt and bicarbonate of soda into a bowl, then rub in the butter. Stir in the currants and sugar and make a well in the centre. Pour in the milk and mix to a soft dough. Turn out on a lightly floured board and knead briefly until smooth. Shape into a round, flatten slightly and cut a deep cross in the dough, almost dividing it into four quarters. Place on a greased baking sheet and bake in the oven for about 30 minutes until hollow-sounding when tapped on the base. Cool on a wire rack.

WHOLESOME WHEATEN BANNOCK

———

Preheat the oven to 180°C/350°F/gas mark 4. Sift the flour, baking powder, bicarbonate of soda and salt into a bowl, then rub in the butter and stir in the herbs. Make a well in the centre, pour in the buttermilk and egg and mix to a soft dough. Turn on to a lightly floured board and knead briefly until smooth. Dust with the plain flour, then turn into a greased 450 g/1 lb loaf tin and bake in the oven for 30 minutes. Reduce the oven temperature to 160°C/325°F/gas mark 3 and bake for a further 15 minutes until hollow-sounding when tapped on the base. Cool on a wire rack.

MAKES
one 450 g/1 lb loaf

450 g/1 lb/4 cups wholemeal (wholewheat) flour

4 teaspoons baking powder

1 teaspoon bicarbonate of soda (baking soda)

1 teaspoon salt

75 g/3 oz/⅓ cup butter

1 teaspoon finely chopped fresh sage

½ teaspoon finely chopped fresh thyme

300 ml/½ pint/1¼ cups buttermilk

1 egg, beaten

1 tablespoon plain (all-purpose) flour

NOURISHING
WHOLEMEAL BREAD

———

MAKES

one 450 g/1 lb loaf

**2 teaspoons black treacle
(molasses)**

**50 ml/2 fl oz/3½ tablespoons
warm water**

**25 g/1 oz/2 tablespoons fresh
baker's yeast**

**450 g/1 lb/4 cups wholemeal
(wholewheat) flour**

1 teaspoon salt

300 ml/½ pint/1¼ cups warm water

Mix together the treacle and warm water, then crumble in the yeast and leave to stand in a warm place for about 10 minutes until frothy. Mix together the flour and salt in a warm bowl and make a well in the centre. Add the yeast mixture and the remaining warm water and mix to a soft, fairly wet dough. Turn out on a lightly floured board and knead briefly until smooth. Turn into a greased 450 g/1 lb loaf tin, cover with a warmed cloth and leave to stand in a warm place for 30 minutes until the dough has doubled in size. Preheat the oven to 190°C/375°/gas mark 5. Remove the cloth and bake the bread in the oven for about 35 minutes until browned on top and hollow-sounding when tapped on the base. Cool on a wire rack.

SIMPLE DROPPED SCONES

Mix together the flour, bicarbonate of soda and sugar in a bowl and make a well in the centre. Add the egg and gradually stir in the buttermilk until you have a thick, smooth batter. Heat the butter in a heavy-based frying pan. Drop spoonfuls of the batter on to the hot pan and cook for 2–3 minutes on each side until golden. Remove from the pan and serve warm.

**225 g/8 oz/2 cups plain
(all-purpose) flour**

**½ teaspoon bicarbonate of soda
(baking soda)**

**1 tablespoon caster (superfine)
sugar**

1 egg, beaten

300 ml/½ pint/1¼ cups buttermilk

25 g/1 oz/2 tablespoons butter

225 g/8 oz/2 cups wholemeal
(wholewheat) flour

2 teaspoons salt

½ teaspoon bicarbonate of soda
(baking soda)

50 g/2 oz/¼ cup butter

2 teaspoons dried basil

1 teaspoon dried oregano

75 g/3 oz/¾ cup hard Irish cheese,
grated

1 tablespoon tomato purée (paste)
or ketchup

1 tablespoon milk

150 ml/¼ pint/⅔ cup buttermilk

COUNTRY HERB SCONES

Oregano (Origanum vulgare) *is the common form of marjoram and grows wild in Ireland. It is a versatile herb that is often used in soups and stews and is also used medicinally as a sedative. It works well in these country scones or with any meat, poultry, game, egg or cheese dishes.*

Preheat the oven to 200°C/400°F/gas mark 6. Sift the flour, salt and bicarbonate of soda into a bowl, then rub in the butter. Stir in the herbs and half the cheese and make a well in the centre. Blend the tomato purée or ketchup into the milk, then add to the flour mixture with the buttermilk and mix to a firm dough. Turn out on a lightly floured board and roll out to 2 cm (½ inch) thick. Cut into 8–10 rounds with a pastry cutter, place on a greased baking sheet and sprinkle with the remaining cheese. Bake in the oven for 20 minutes until risen but not hard on top. Serve warm or cool with butter or cream.

BARM BRACK

Barm is the name for the frothy yeast that appears on the top of fermenting malt liquors and ale barm was commonly used as the raising agent for baking in early Irish cookery. This recipe is for a traditional type of cake mix, but often serves as a bread when it is cut into slices and served with butter or cream.

Stir the yeast and 1 teaspoon of the sugar into the warm milk and leave in a warm place for 20 minutes until frothy. Put the flour in a bowl and stir in the caraway seeds, allspice and salt. Rub in the butter and make a well in the centre. Pour in the yeast mixture and the eggs and knead to a soft dough, folding in the fruit. Turn on to a lightly floured board and knead briefly, then place in a greased bowl, cover with a damp cloth and leave in a warm place for 1 hour until it has doubled in size. Preheat the oven to 200°C/400°F/gas mark 6. Divide between two greased loaf tins and bake in the oven for 1 hour. Dissolve the remaining sugar in a little boiling water to make a syrup, then brush this over the warm loaves and return to the oven for 3 minutes to glaze.

20 g/¾ oz/1¼ tablespoons
fresh yeast

150 g/5 oz/⅔ cup caster
(superfine) sugar

300 ml/½ pint/1¼ cups warm milk

450 g/1 lb/4 cups plain
(all-purpose) flour

1 tablespoon caraway seeds

1 teaspoon allspice

¼ teaspoon salt

50 g/2 oz/¼ cup butter

2 eggs, lightly beaten

225 g/8 oz/1⅓ cups sultanas
(golden raisins)

175 g/6 oz/1 cup currants

50 g/2 oz/⅓ cup chopped mixed
(candied) peel

Soups and Stews

In most peasant societies, the traditional main meal of the day was dispensed from the soup or stew pot which simmered over the stove during the day. There was no real distinction between a soup and a stew, as they were as hearty and robust as the people could afford to make them, adding whatever ingredients were available at the time – hence the expression 'pot luck'.

If a choice of ingredients was available, they would make dishes like the still-famous Dankey stew. 'Dankey' means slightly drunk, so it is not surprising that one of the main ingredients of this stew is a hefty measure of Irish stout. Since this not only adds a rich flavour but also tenderises the meat, it was often added to stews, especially at a time when the water was not always safe to drink and everyone in the family would tend to drink beer of one kind or another.

Because most farmers kept cows and made their own butter and cream, these were also common ingredients of soups and stews.

A pot was never boiled by beauty.

———

Old Irish saying

During the Great Famine, soup kitchens proliferated throughout Ireland and many people relied entirely on their daily quota of this free soup for survival when their potato crops were hit by the blight. It was Alexis Soyer, the chef at London's Reform Club in Pall Mall, London, who wrote the official recipe for the universally dispensed soup. During 1848 alone, a total of 8,750 men, women and children were sustained daily on Soyer's soup.

TRADITIONAL POTATO SOUP

SERVES

4

Melt the butter in a large saucepan and gently fry the onions until translucent. Add the potatoes and carrot, then stir in the stock and milk. Add the bay leaf, parsley and thyme, and season with salt and pepper. Bring to a simmer, then simmer gently for about 1 hour. Discard the bay leaf and liquidize the soup, then return it to the pan and reheat. Serve with a swirl of cream and garnish with the chives.

50 g/2 oz/¼ cup butter

2 onions, sliced

900 g/2 lb potatoes, sliced

1 carrot, sliced

1.2 litres/2 pints/5 cups stock

600 ml/1 pint/2½ cups milk

1 bay leaf

1 teaspoon chopped fresh parsley

½ teaspoon chopped fresh thyme

salt and freshly ground black pepper

2 tablespoons single (light) cream

1 tablespoon finely chopped chives

SERVES

4

LEEK AND OATMEAL BROTH

600 ml/1 pint/2½ cups milk

25 g/1 oz/2 tablespoons butter

2 tablespoons oatmeal

3 large leeks, cut into chunks

½ teaspoon salt

¼ teaspoon white pepper

½ tablespoon chopped fresh parsley

Place the milk and butter in a large saucepan and heat until the butter has melted. Stir in the oatmeal and simmer for 1 minute, stirring continuously, then add the leeks, salt and pepper. Cover and simmer over a low heat for about 40 minutes. Add the parsley and simmer for a further 3 minutes before serving.

BLUE CHEESE SOUP

———

Heat the oil in a large saucepan and gently sauté the bacon for 1 minute. Add the shallots, courgette and potatoes, cover the pan and cook gently for about 15 minutes until the vegetables are soft. Stir in the stock, bring to the boil, then simmer for 10 minutes. Remove from the heat and leave to cool slightly. Liquidize the soup, then return it to the saucepan. Stir in the cheese and cream and heat through gently. Sprinkle with pepper and serve garnished with the parsley.

2 teaspoons vegetable oil

6 streaky bacon rashers (slices), rinded and chopped

3 shallots, chopped

1 large courgette (zucchini), sliced

3 potatoes, diced

1.2 litres/2 pints/5 cups stock

75 g/3 oz/¾ cup blue Irish cheese, crumbled

150 ml/¼ pint/⅔ cup single (light) cream

¼ teaspoon freshly ground black pepper

2 tablespoons finely chopped fresh parsley

SERVES

4

25 g/1 oz/2 tablespoons butter

1 onion, finely chopped

2 potatoes, finely chopped

450 g/1 lb nettle tips, well washed

**375 ml/13 fl oz/1½ cups
vegetable stock**

250 ml/8 fl oz/1 cup milk

1 teaspoon salt

**½ teaspoon freshly ground
black pepper**

6 tablespoons single (light) cream

IRISH NETTLE SOUP

Nettles (Urtica dioica) *have long been used as a vegetable in Ireland. Any fresh young nettles can be used, but roadside nettles should be avoided as these will be heavily polluted. The tender and flavoursome tips of young nettles are washed, cooked for 10 minutes in the water which is left on the leaves, then roughly chopped, seasoned with salt and pepper and served with a knob of butter. Rich in iron, they have a slightly bitter taste and have been made into this milk-based nettle soup since as early as the sixth century. The Irish also make a nettle tea, which is used to treat arthritis, as a blood purifier and, oddly enough considering its stinging qualities, to treat skin disorders.*

Melt the butter in a large saucepan and cook the onion and potatoes for about 5 minutes until soft, stirring occasionally. Add the washed nettles and cook for 3 minutes until the leaves wilt, stirring the ingredients together. Stir in the stock, milk, salt and pepper. Bring to the boil, cover and simmer for 15 minutes until the potatoes are tender. Liquidize the soup, then return it to the saucepan and reheat gently. Serve with the cream spooned on top.

POTATO AND CHERVIL SOUP

———

SERVES
4

Potato soup is best made with floury, rather than waxy, potatoes, and one of the best varieties is Maris Piper. This version is flavoured with chervil, which is a popular culinary herb in Ireland. The 30 cm (12 inch) high chervil plant (Anthriscus cerefolium) has fern-like leaves which taste mildly of anise. In Irish country remedies, the leaves are used medicinally to reduce fevers and as a mild diuretic.

Melt the butter in a large saucepan and sauté the onions for about 5 minutes until soft. Add the potatoes, stock and bouquet garni and bring to the boil. Chop the stalks from the chervil, add these to the saucepan and simmer for 20 minutes. Remove from the heat, discard the bouquet garni and leave to cool slightly. Liquidize the soup, then return it to the pan. Chop the chervil leaves finely. Reserve a spoonful for garnish, add the rest to the saucepan and season with salt and pepper. Reheat gently and serve with a swirl of cream and a sprinkling of chervil leaves.

75 g/3 oz/⅓ cup butter

2 large onions, chopped

450 g/1 lb potatoes, diced

1.75 ml/3 pints/7½ cups vegetable stock

1 bouquet garni

175 g/6 oz fresh chervil

½ teaspoon salt and white pepper

4 tablespoons double (heavy) or whipping cream, whipped

SERVES

4

50 g/2 oz/¼ cup butter
1 large onion, sliced
275 g/10 oz carrots, chopped
1.2 litres/2 pints/5 cups
vegetable stock
150 ml/¼ pint/⅔ cup orange juice
¼ teaspoon salt and white pepper
1 tablespoon single (light) cream
1 teaspoon chopped fresh chives

CELTIC CARROT SOUP

The carrot is a familiar root vegetable which complements all manner of foods. Apart from its phallic shape and colour, since Classical times, and probably even before that, carrots were known aphrodisiacs and in fact it is now known that the iron, sugar and vitamins A, B and C that they contain help to restore the nervous system and promote sexual activity. 'Carrot top' was once used as a nickname for Irish people with red hair – even though the top of a carrot is strictly speaking as green as the meadows of Ireland!

Melt half the butter in a large saucepan and sauté the onion for about 5 minutes until soft. Add the carrots and cook for 2 minutes. Stir in the stock and bring to the boil. Cover and simmer for 30 minutes until the carrots are tender. Leave to cool slightly, then liquidize the soup and return it to the saucepan. Add the orange juice, salt and pepper and bring gently to the boil, stirring in the remaining butter until melted into the soup. Serve garnished with cream and chives.

BRALLION CLAM CHOWDER

Brallion are among the finest Irish clams, but you can use any fresh clams for this recipe.

Place the clams in a large saucepan and cover with water. Bring to the boil over a high heat, cover and cook for about 4 minutes just until they open. Discard any that remain closed. Remove the clams with a slotted spoon, remove the shells and dice the meat. Strain the cooking liquor, return it to the pan and add the potatoes, milk and butter. Bring to the boil, then simmer for 30 minutes. Add the chives and simmer for a further 15 minutes. Mix the flour into a paste with a little water, then stir the paste into the soup and stir until thickened. Return the clams to the soup and heat through before serving bubbling hot.

24 Irish Brallion clams, washed
4 potatoes, finely diced
600 ml/1 pint/2½ cups milk
25 g/1 oz/2 tablespoons butter
2 tablespoons chopped fresh chives
2 tablespoons plain (all-purpose) flour

GAELIC SHRIMP CHOWDER

SERVES
4

25 g/1 oz/2 tablespoons butter

1 large onion, sliced

3 potatoes, sliced

150 ml/¼ pint/⅔ cup boiling water

¼ teaspoon salt

¼ teaspoon freshly ground
black pepper

600 ml/1 pint/2½ cups shrimps
or prawns, shelled

600 ml/1 pint/2½ cups milk

50 g/2 oz/½ cup hard Irish cheese,
grated

½ tablespoon finely chopped
fresh parsley

Melt the butter in a large saucepan and sauté the onion for a few minutes until translucent. Add the potatoes and stir until coated, then add the water, salt and pepper. Bring to the boil, cover and simmer for 15 minutes until the potatoes are tender. Add the shrimps and milk, return to the boil and stir in the cheese and parsley. Simmer gently for 5 minutes, then serve hot.

COCKLER'S SOUP

SERVES

4

Place the cockles in a large saucepan with the stock, wine or water, bring to the boil, cover and steam for about 4 minutes, shaking the pan occasionally until the shells have opened. Lift out the cockles with a slotted spoon, remove the meat and discard the shells. Strain and reserve the cooking broth. Melt the butter in the pan, stir in the flour and cook for 1 minute, stirring. Add the strained broth and stir until smooth. Add the milk, celery, parsley, lemon juice, salt and pepper. Bring to the boil and cook over a low heat for 8 minutes, stirring occasionally. Add the cockles and cook for 3 minutes. Serve with a dash of cream on top.

48 cockles, scrubbed

150 ml/¼ pint/⅔ cup stock, wine or water

50 g/2 oz/¼ cup butter

2 tablespoons plain (all-purpose) flour

600 ml/1 pint/2½ cups milk

2 celery sticks (stalks), chopped

1 tablespoon finely chopped fresh parsley

juice of 1 lemon

1 teaspoon salt

½ teaspoon freshly ground black pepper

4 tablespoons double (heavy) cream

EIRAAN LAMB AND CHEESE SOUP

SERVES

4

900 g/2 lb lamb chops on the bone

1 large onion, finely chopped

3 garlic cloves, finely chopped

2 bay leaves

1.2 litres/2 pints/5 cups water

25 g/1 oz/2 tablespoons butter

25 g/1 oz/¼ cup plain
(all-purpose) flour

1.2 litres/2 pints/5 cups milk

100 g/4 oz/1 cup Irish Farmhouse
cheese, grated

4 carrots, diced

2 leeks, finely chopped

3 potatoes, diced

½ teaspoon salt

½ teaspoon freshly ground
black pepper

½ tablespoon chopped fresh chives

Bay (Laurus nobilis) *was one of the earliest herbs to be used in cooking and was brought to Ireland from southern Europe. The leaves are usually used dried, as fresh leaves can be slightly bitter. Besides its distinctive flavour, bay is supposed to stimulate the appetite and encourage digestion.*

Put the chops, onion, garlic, bay leaves and water in a large saucepan, bring to the boil, then cover and simmer for 1 hour. Remove the chops from the pan, discard the bones and cut the meat into small pieces. Strain and reserve the stock, discarding the vegetables. Melt the butter in a clean saucepan, stir in the flour and cook for 1 minute, stirring continuously. Stir in the milk, bring to the boil, then simmer for 2 minutes, stirring. Add the reserved lamb and stock, the cheese and vegetables, return to the boil, then simmer for 30 minutes, stirring occasionally. Season with salt and pepper and serve sprinkled with chives.

CROFTER'S HAM, BACON AND BEAN SOUP

SERVES
4

Drain and rinse the beans, then put them in a large saucepan with the ham, cover with cold water, bring to the boil, then cover and simmer for 2 hours. Remove the hock from the saucepan with a slotted spoon. Discard the fat and bones, dice the meat and return it to the saucepan. Heat the oil in a frying pan and sauté the bacon, onion, garlic, celery, carrots, bay leaves and cumin for about 5 minutes until soft. Add to the ham with the tomatoes, vinegar, water, mustard and pepper. Bring to the boil, then cover and simmer for about 1½ hours until all the ingredients are tender.

225 g/8 oz/1 cup dried haricot (navy) beans, soaked overnight in cold water

225 g/8 oz ham hock on the bone

1 tablespoon vegetable oil

50 g/2 oz streaky bacon, rinded and diced

1 large onion, finely chopped

3 garlic cloves, chopped

2 celery sticks (stalks), chopped

2 large carrots, chopped

2 bay leaves

2 teaspoons ground cumin

6 tomatoes, peeled and chopped

2 tablespoons balsamic or wine vinegar

1.2 litres/2 pints/5 cups water

1 teaspoon mustard

1 teaspoon black pepper

DANKEY STEW

3 celery sticks (stalks), chopped

2 carrots, sliced

2 large scrag end of mutton chops

2 onions, quartered

1 tablespoon mushroom ketchup

600 ml/1 pint/2½ cups Irish stout

¼ teaspoon salt

¼ teaspoon freshly ground
black pepper

2 potatoes, sliced

50 g/2 oz/¼ cup pearl barley,
soaked in a cup of cold water

25 g/1 oz/2 tablespoons
salted butter

The generous quantity of Irish stout is what gives this stew its name, which means 'slightly drunk'. Since the traditional mutton is no longer readily available, you can use lamb for this recipe; you may need to reduce the cooking time slightly.

Arrange the celery and carrots in the bottom of a large flameproof casserole dish, place the meat on top and finish with the onions. Stir the mushroom ketchup into the stout, then pour it over the ingredients and season with salt and pepper. Cover with layers of potato slices. Bring to the boil, then cover and simmer at the lowest possible heat for about 1 hour, or cook in a preheated oven at 150°C/300°F/gas mark 2 for 1 hour. Add the barley into the stew and cook for a further 1 hour. Stir in the butter and allow it to melt before serving.

RUSTIC LAMB HOT POT
WITH PARSLEY DUMPLINGS

SERVES

4

This is a delicious lamb and vegetable stew that is perfectly complemented by the dumplings seasoned with locally grown parsley. Parsley has been used in Irish cooking since it was introduced from southern Europe during the sixteenth century. You can also serve the dumplings with any stew or casserole.

Put the lamb and bones in a large saucepan, cover with cold water and bring to the boil. Skim off the scum that rises to the surface. Add all the vegetables except the cabbage, season with salt and pepper and top up with water. Return to the boil, cover and simmer gently for about 1 hour until the meat is tender. Lift out and discard the bones. Add the Worcestershire sauce. Ladle out 300 ml/½ pint/1¼ cups of the liquid and mix it with the cream, then return this to the saucepan and add the cabbage. Simmer for about 10 minutes until the cabbage is heated through.

900 g/2 lb shoulder of lamb, trimmed and diced

bones from the lamb

2 carrots, chopped

1 onion, sliced

2 small white turnips, chopped

4 potatoes, sliced

2 celery sticks (stalks), chopped

1 leek, thinly sliced

¼ teaspoon salt

¼ teaspoon freshly ground black pepper

a dash of Worcestershire sauce

150 ml/¼ pint/⅔ cup single (light) cream

¼ white cabbage, finely shredded

1 tablespoon finely chopped fresh parsley

For the parsley dumplings

100 g/4 oz/1 cup self-raising (self-rising) flour

1 tablespoon finely chopped fresh parsley

¼ teaspoon salt

¼ teaspoon freshly ground black pepper

50 g/2 oz/¼ cup shredded suet

about 3 tablespoons water

To make the dumplings, mix the flour with the parsley, salt and pepper, then stir in the suet. Add just enough water to mix to a stiff dough, then shape with floured hands into eight dumplings.

Lift the meat and vegetables out of the saucepan with a slotted spoon and keep them warm. Add the dumplings to the liquid, cover and simmer for about 25 minutes until the dumplings are cooked through. Return the meat and vegetables to the saucepan to reheat, then serve in deep plates sprinkled with the parsley.

TRADITIONAL IRISH STEW

SERVES

4

Lamb can be substituted for the traditional mutton in this classic recipe. It has a slightly milder flavour but will be equally delicious. You can also serve the dish with parsley dumplings, cooking them in the same way as for the Rustic Lamb Hot Pot (page 35).

Cut the excess fat off the mutton pieces and sauté the fat pieces in a casserole dish until the fat is released. Lift out the remaining fat pieces with a slotted spoon and discard. Season the flour with half the salt and pepper and toss the remaining meat in the seasoned flour. Add them to the dish and fry until browned on all sides. Lift out three-quarters of the meat, leaving a layer of meat at the bottom of the dish. Cover with a quarter of the onion slices, followed by a quarter of the carrots, then a quarter of the leeks. Season with a little of the salt and pepper, then add a quarter of the potatoes. Continue layering and seasoning until all the ingredients have been used, adding the pearl barley and thyme before the final layer of potatoes. Stir the parsley into the stock and pour over the stew, then spoon over the butter. Bring to the boil for 3 minutes and skim off any scum, then reduce the heat, cover and simmer for about 2 hours until all the meat and vegetables are very tender.

900 g/2 lb scrag end and neck of mutton, chopped into pieces

2 tablespoons plain (all-purpose) flour

½ teaspoon salt

½ teaspoon freshly ground black pepper

3 onions, sliced

4 carrots, sliced

2 leeks, sliced

5 potatoes, thickly sliced

1 tablespoon pearl barley

1 teaspoon finely chopped fresh thyme leaves

1 tablespoon finely chopped fresh parsley

900 ml/1½ pints/3¾ cups stock

1 tablespoon butter, melted

SERVES

4

SIMPLE IRISH STEW

1 kg/2¼ lb middle neck of lamb,
cut into chunks

2 large onions, thinly sliced

1 kg/2¼ lb potatoes, thinly sliced

1 teaspoon finely chopped
fresh marjoram

½ teaspoon salt

½ teaspoon freshly ground
black pepper

1.2 litres/2 pints/5 cups mutton
or lamb stock

½ teaspoon finely chopped
fresh rosemary

½ teaspoon finely chopped
fresh parsley

This is a simple version of Irish stew using rosemary (Rosmarinus officinalis), a popular herb that grows wild in Ireland and is particularly good with both lamb and pork dishes. It is said to improve the memory, and an oil derived from rosemary is made into a tonic for digestive, nervous and circulatory problems, headaches and arthritis. You can cook the stew on top of the stove, then simply brown it in the oven if you prefer.

Preheat the oven to 160°C/325°F/gas mark 3. Trim the fat from the lamb pieces. In a large flameproof casserole dish, layer the meat, onions and potatoes alternately, sprinkling each layer with a little marjoram, salt and pepper and finishing with a layer of potatoes. Add enough stock to half-fill the casserole and sprinkle in the rosemary. Bring to the boil, cover and cook in the oven for about 2 hours. Remove the lid, increase the oven temperature to 190°C/375°F/gas mark 5 and return to the oven for 30 minutes to brown the potato topping. Serve sprinkled with parsley.

WHITE IRISH STEW

There are many forms of Irish stew and every cook has their own favourite combination of ingredients, most of which are traditionally based on mutton, although lamb is now more commonly used. The long cooking of the potatoes and onions makes this dish thick and creamy. It is sometimes served with pickled cabbage.

Preheat the oven to 150°C/300°F/gas mark 2. Set aside a quarter of the potatoes in salted water. Arrange a layer of potatoes in the base of a greased casserole dish and cover with a layer of meat, then a layer of onion slices. Repeat the layers until all the potatoes, meat and onions are used, seasoning as you go. Pour in the stock and milk, cover and cook in the oven for about 1¾ hours. Drain the reserved potatoes. Remove the casserole from the oven and cover with a layer of the reserved potatoes. Pour over the melted butter and return to the oven for a further 1 hour until the potatoes are golden.

1.5 kg/3 lb potatoes, sliced
700 g/1½ lb mutton chops
450 g/1 lb onions, thickly sliced
¼ teaspoon salt
¼ teaspoon freshly ground black pepper
600 ml/1 pint/2½ cups lamb stock
150 ml/¼ pint/⅔ cup milk
50 g/2 oz/¼ cup butter, melted

39

VEAL CODDLE

SERVES
6

6 veal escalopes

25 g/1 oz veal

50 g/2 oz cooked ham

100 g/4 oz pork sausage meat

1 garlic clove, crushed

¼ teaspoon salt

¼ teaspoon freshly ground
black pepper

1 egg yolk, beaten

1½ tablespoons plain (all-purpose)
flour

25 g/1 oz/2 tablespoons butter

Preheat the oven to 180°C/350°F/gas mark 4. Beat the veal escalopes flat with a rolling pin. Mince together the veal, cooked ham and sausage meat and stir in the garlic, salt and pepper. Shape into six sausages, roll them in the veal slices and tie with cooks' string. Dip in the egg yolk, then in the flour. Heat the butter in a frying pan and sauté for 15 minutes until golden brown. Transfer to an ovenproof dish and cook in the oven for 15 minutes while you prepare the sauces.

To make the tomato sauce, melt the butter in a small saucepan and sauté the onion for about 5 minutes until soft. Stir in the remaining ingredients, bring to the boil, then simmer for about 10 minutes until thickened. To make the cheese sauce, mix together all the ingredients and cook over a gentle heat for a few minutes until well blended, stirring continuously.

Remove the string from the rolls. Pour over the tomato sauce, then the cheese sauce and either return to the oven or place under the grill until golden brown on top.

For the tomato sauce

30 g/1½ oz/3 tablespoons butter

1 onion, finely chopped

400 g/14 oz/1 large can
of tomatoes

1 garlic clove, crushed

½ teaspoon salt

½ teaspoon freshly ground
black pepper

For the cheese sauce

50 g/2 oz/½ cup hard Irish cheese,
grated

300 ml/½ pint/1¼ cups single
(light) cream

1 teaspoon arrowroot

½ teaspoon ground turmeric

SERVES

4

DUBLIN CODDLE

8 thick slices of ham, cut into chunks

16 thin pork sausages

900 g/2 lb potatoes, sliced

4 large onions, chopped

4 tablespoons chopped fresh parsley

¼ teaspoon salt

¼ teaspoon freshly ground black pepper

Place the ham and sausages in a large saucepan, cover with water and bring to the boil. Boil for 5 minutes, then strain, reserving the liquid. Return the ham and sausages to the saucepan and cover with layers of potatoes, onions and parsley, seasoning the layers with salt and pepper. Pour over enough of the reserved liquid to cover the ingredients. Bring to the boil, cover and simmer for 45 minutes. Remove the lid and continue to simmer for a further 20 minutes or so until the liquid has reduced by half.

BACON, BEEF
AND BEAN CODDLE

Drain and rinse the beans thoroughly. Place in a pan, cover with the stock, bring to the boil and boil for 10 minutes. Heat the oil in a large saucepan and sauté the bacon, beef, onion, garlic, celery, carrots, bay leaves and cumin for about 5 minutes until soft. Add the beans and stock, the mushrooms, tomatoes, vinegar, and salt and pepper to taste. Bring to the boil, then cover and simmer for 1½ hours until tender. Remove the bay leaves before serving.

**225 g/8 oz/1⅓ cups dried cannellini
or other white beans, soaked
overnight in cold water**

1.2 litres/2 pints/5 cups stock

1 tablespoon vegetable oil

**50 g/2 oz streaky bacon, rinded
and diced**

225 g/8 oz shin of beef, diced

1 onion, finely chopped

3 garlic cloves, chopped

3 celery sticks (stalks), chopped

2 carrots, chopped

2 bay leaves

3 teaspoons ground cumin

2 field mushrooms, chopped

3 tomatoes, peeled and chopped

2 tablespoons malt vinegar

salt and freshly ground black pepper

BACON AND CABBAGE STEW

SERVES

4

50 g/2 oz/¼ cup butter

1 medium-sized cabbage, shredded

1.75 litres/3 pints/7½ cups stock

1 shallot or small onion,
finely chopped

1 bay leaf

¼ teaspoon salt

¼ teaspoon freshly ground
black pepper

4 streaky bacon rashers (slices),
rinded and chopped

100 g/4 oz pork sausages, sliced
into chunks

1 eating (dessert) apple, peeled,
cored and chopped

Melt the butter in a large saucepan, add the cabbage and stir over a low heat for 10 minutes until the cabbage has wilted. Add the stock, shallot or onion, bay leaf, salt and pepper, bring to the boil, then simmer for about 10 minutes until cabbage is tender. Add the bacon and sausages and simmer for a further 10 minutes. Add the apple and continue simmering for 15 minutes. Remove the bay leaf before serving.

SHEBEEN BACON AND POTATO SUPPER

SERVES

4

Put the sausages, bacon and stock in a flameproof casserole dish, bring to the boil, then simmer for 5 minutes. Add all the remaining ingredients except the chives, and bring back to the boil. Cover and simmer gently for 1 hour, stirring occasionally, until the stew has thickened. Sprinkle the chives over the top and serve immediately.

450 g/1 lb pork sausages

8 thick back bacon rashers (slices)

**1.2 litres/2 pints/5 cups
vegetable stock**

8 potatoes, sliced

4 onions, sliced

**3 tablespoons chopped fresh
parsley**

¼ teaspoon salt

**¼ teaspoon freshly ground
black pepper**

**2 teaspoons finely chopped
fresh chives**

Seafood

There is evidence from ancient kitchen middens, or large rubbish heaps, around the city of Cork, of a thriving trade in oysters going back to the Stone Age, and the many oyster fairs held throughout the country celebrate a ritual going back to Ireland's earliest settlers. Mussels have similarly been collected for food since ancient times, and the Murphy's International Mussel Fair, held annually in Bantry Bay, celebrates the seafood's long history. Although plentiful in Ireland, mussels are highly regarded in France, especially in the north-west, an area which has long links with Ireland. This is no better demonstrated than at the French Festival, held in July, which celebrates the long cultural links between Dun Laoghaire and Brest in France.

In 1734, a woman known as Molly Malone was buried in St John's Churchyard, south-east of Dublin, at Blackrock. This is said to be the Molly of the famous rhyme, who wheeled her wheelbarrow through Dublin's

Mussels are the food of kings; limpets are the food of peasants.

———

Old Irish saying

broad and narrow streets, selling cockles and mussels, 'alive, alive-oh'. At the bottom of Grafton Street in Dublin, there is a statue of the voluptuous Molly, together with her well-stocked barrow.

Some of the best mussels in the whole of Ireland are found on the wild coasts of the west of the island, and these are now commercially packaged and exported around the world. The people of County Kildare swear by their local mussels, which come from Bannow Bay, and they buy them by weight in the local markets.

Ireland's coastal waters provide ideal conditions in which clams thrive. To the west of Ireland are the deeps of the Atlantic Ocean, and to the east are the shallower waters of the Irish Sea. Around ten types of native clam are to be found in the seas around Ireland. Most of these are quite small, but the large hardshell clam has been introduced from its native North America into the waters around the south coast of Ireland. In Northern Ireland, the name for the soft-shelled clam – which is the largest of the local species found in Ireland – is Brallion. There are still many cocklers around Ireland's sandy coasts, raking the flats for the sought-after clams and cockles.

The local fishermen around Derrynane harbour in County Kerry have an odd method of ensnaring the delicious razorfish, which bury themselves in the soft sand when the tide goes out. Razorfish have long, thin, sharp shells and usually have to be dug out of the sand with a pronged rake. In Derrynane, the locals sprinkle salt on the sand where small holes reveal the presence of razorfish. The intensity of the salt causes the shellfish to propel themselves out of their lairs, and they are caught as they leap into the air!

Ireland is famous for its oysters, and when Charles Dickens was writing about being 'secret, and self-contained, and solitary as an oyster' in *A Christmas Carol*, they were the fare of the Victorian poor. Some of Ireland's best and most succulent small oysters come from the areas of Kilcolgan in County Galway, from Galway Bay itself, Kenmare, Clarinbridge off the west coast, and Strangford Lough. A Pacific variety, known as gigas, is also available. Although it is traditional to eat Irish oysters raw with a drop of lemon juice and a thick slice of soda bread, all washed down with a favourite Irish stout, they can be grilled, steamed or sautéed. St Patrick's Day, 17 March, falls conveniently in the middle of the local oyster season. Although a usual serving would be about six to eight oysters per person, Casanova is reputed to have consumed 50 oysters every morning! Whether that confirms their aphrodisiac qualities, you can decide for yourself. Freshly smoked or canned smoked oysters are also on sale in some fishmongers.

Dublin Bay prawns are also known as the Norway lobster. The reddish-orange or pink prawn has a body around 20 cm (8 inches) in length, with long, narrow, striped claws. Dublin Bay prawns do not change colour when cooked, unlike other crustaceans. This marine crustacean, the source of scampi, does not come from Dublin Bay at all, but is found in Atlantic waters. The name comes from the fact that the Dublin fishing fleet sailed into port with a quantity of these prawns mixed in with their catch. The fishermen would then distribute the prawns to itinerant street-vendors as they had no value in the fish markets, so the name came from the bay from where the street-vendors got their wares.

Lobsters are also a delicacy in Irish fish markets and are sold live and fresh, resplendent in their blue-black shells. Lobsters are quite expensive, however, which could be why the famous Irish lobster dish became known as Dublin Lawyer!

The shrimp found in the waters around Ireland are brown shrimp and are generally less than half the size of the smallest prawns. However, as with the prawns, shrimp are now highly valued in Ireland.

Although strictly speaking it should appear in the vegetables chapter, another Irish delicacy that feels more at home in a chapter about the sea is carragheen, the reddish seaweed which comes in two varieties: stack-house and sloke or *slugane* (*Porphyra umbilicalis*). Sloke is known as laver in Wales where they make the jelly-like substance called laverbread. In the National Gallery in Dublin, there is evidence of the reverence that even the Irish aristocracy had for sloke, as one Georgian exhibit is a beautiful silver sloke pot with a long wooden handle. Another variety of this edible seaweed is called by its Latin name, *Porphyra purpurae*, which means 'purple giant'. When cooked, this red-tinged seaweed turns a greenish colour. It is often used as a vegetable, or can be added fresh to salads. Sloke is usually sold already boiled for several hours, when it turns out as a dark-green mush. It is then usually cooked again in milk, then pressed to remove as much moisture as possible, making it somewhat like well-cooked spinach. After this, it is finely chopped, mixed or coated with oatmeal, and fried with bacon or in bacon fat until golden brown on both sides.

All seaweeds contain gelatinous agar-agar, a thickening agent used as a substitute for gelatine by vegetarians. Seaweeds will keep for years if dried and bleached, and are said to ease indigestion and aid sleep. Some seaweeds are used in Irish cooking for thickening fish stews and soups. They are usually bought dried, and must be washed and cleaned of grit before cooking. In County Donegal and on the shores of Ulster, another form of edible seaweed is known locally as dulse or *dilisk*, deriving its Latin name, *Palmaria palmata*, from its frond-like shape.

MOLLY'S ONION MUSSELS

———

If possible, leave mussels or other shellfish in a container of fresh seawater or salt water to purge before eating or cooking, then soak them in cold water for about an hour, discarding any that float, are broken, or do not close when tapped sharply. Scrub the shells clean and remove any barnacles and weed, then cut off the beards with a knife.

Put the mussels, water and wine in a saucepan over a high heat, cover and cook for about 5 minutes until the mussels open, shaking the pan occasionally. Discard any that remain closed, lift the mussels from the pan with a slotted spoon and strain and reserve the cooking liquor. Melt the butter in a saucepan and sauté the onions for a few minutes until soft. Add the shallots and garlic, then the potatoes, celery, chicory and carrot. Tie the thyme, bay leaf and parsley together with string, then add to the pan with the mussel liquor and season with pepper. Cover and simmer for 1 hour. Remove the lid and return the mussels to the pan to heat through for about 2 minutes before serving.

30 fresh mussels, scrubbed

120 ml/4 fl oz/½ cup water

120 ml/4 fl oz/½ cup white wine

1 tablespoon butter

6 large onions, sliced

4 shallots, chopped

5 garlic cloves

3 potatoes, sliced

2 celery sticks (stalks), chopped

6 chicory leaves (Belgian endive), chopped

1 carrot, chopped

1 sprig of thyme

1 bay leaf

1 sprig of fresh parsley

¼ teaspoon freshly ground black pepper

SERVES

4

MACHA'S MUSSELS

1.5 kg/3 lb fresh mussels, scrubbed
3 tablespoons water
25 g/1 oz/2 tablespoons butter
2 shallots, finely chopped
1 bay leaf
a handful of chopped fresh parsley
150 ml/¼ pint/⅔ cup Irish cider
150 ml/¼ pint/⅔ cup single
(light) cream

Although mussels can be eaten raw, the traditional method of serving was to cook them first on a heated stone. This method may be more suitable for the modern Irish kitchen! Prepare the mussels as described on page 53.

Place the mussels in a wide shallow pan with the water over a high heat, cover and cook for about 4 minutes until the mussels open, shaking the pan occasionally. Discard any that remain closed. Remove the mussels from the pan with a slotted spoon and set aside. Melt the butter in a pan and sauté the shallots, bay leaf and half the parsley for a few minutes until soft. Add the mussels and pour in the cider. Cook over a high heat for 2 minutes, shaking occasionally. Remove from the heat and lift out the mussels with a slotted spoon, reserving the liquor in the pan. Add the cream and simmer gently for a few minutes until reduced and thickened. Arrange the mussels on a serving dish, pour over the sauce and garnish with the remaining parsley.

BUTTERED GIGAS OYSTERS

———

SERVES

4

To open oysters you need a strong, sharp, short-bladed oyster knife. Protect your hand with a towel or oven glove and hold the oyster firmly with the flat shell uppermost. Insert the knife at the side next to the hinge and prise the shells apart with a twisting movement. Loosen the flesh from the top shell, then from the bottom shell, discarding any loose pieces of shell.

Open the oysters into a sieve over a bowl to catch the liquor, and pick out any grit or shell from the oysters. Heat half the butter until it is foaming, then toss in the oysters and heat through for about 1 minute. Arrange the buttered toast on a serving plate. Lift the oysters out of the pan and place on the toast. Add the rest of the butter and the reserved liquor to the pan, bring to the boil, then pour over the oysters and serve garnished with the lemon wedges.

24 gigas oysters
100 g/4 oz/½ cup butter
8 slices of hot toast, buttered
1 lemon, cut into wedges

DUBLIN BAY PRAWNS IN CARRAGHEEN JELLY

SERVES

4

a large handful of carragheen,
or Irish seaweed

600 ml/1 pint/2½ cups water

1 bay leaf

2 cloves

2 sprigs of fresh parsley

a pinch of salt

6 cooked Dublin Bay prawns
(saltwater crayfish)

1 teaspoon vinegar

2 slices of lemon

This recipe contains carragheen, or Irish seaweed, as the thickening agent. Named after an Irish village and commonly known as Irish moss, it can be bought dried in delicatessens. As well as in seafood dishes such as this one, it is used in Irish desserts, to clarify beer, in ice-cream, and in cosmetics and medicines. It is said to be a good cure for coughs, colds and indigestion, and is rich in vitamins and minerals.

Soak the carragheen in water for 15 minutes, then drain. Put the carragheen and water in a saucepan with the bay leaf, cloves, 1 parsley sprig and salt. Bring to the boil, then simmer for 1 hour.

To prepare the Dublin Bay prawns, twist apart the body and tail, then gently pull the tail meat out of the shell. Remove and discard the intestinal thread from along the back of the meat. Pull open the body and scrape out the yellow meat. Place all the meat in a bowl.

Stir the vinegar into the carragheen mixture, then strain it over the prawns. Leave to cool, then chill and set. Turn out on to a serving plate and garnish with the remaining parsley and the lemon slices.

PRAWNS
IN COCKTAIL SAUCE

This classic sauce can also be used for crabs, shrimp or lobster tails, and diners squeeze the lime juice over the dish before eating. The dish can also be garnished with a sprig of parsley and a slice or two of lemon. If you buy live prawns or shrimp, drop them into boiling water for a few minutes until they turn pink, then drain and leave to cool. When cool, pinch off the heads and legs and pull the shell away from the body and tail.

Combine the mayonnaise, cream, tomato ketchup, Worcestershire sauce, lime juice, Tabasco sauce, salt and pepper in a bowl and beat until smooth and evenly coloured. Spoon the mixture over the prawns, sprinkle with paprika and cayenne and garnish with the lime quarters.

300 ml/½ pint/1¼ cups mayonnaise

2 tablespoons double (heavy) cream

1 tablespoon tomato ketchup

1 teaspoon Worcestershire sauce

1 teaspoon lime juice

¼ teaspoon Tabasco sauce

a pinch of salt

a pinch of freshly ground black pepper

450 g/1 lb cooked, peeled prawns (shrimp)

1 teaspoon paprika

¼ teaspoon cayenne

2 limes, quartered

CLASSIC DUBLIN BAY PRAWN COCKTAIL

SERVES

4

4 tablespoons whipping cream, whipped

2 teaspoons malt vinegar

2 teaspoons fresh grated horseradish

½ teaspoon tomato purée (paste)

¼ teaspoon Worcestershire sauce

3 drops of Tabasco sauce

salt and freshly ground black pepper

10 cooked Dublin Bay prawn (saltwater crayfish) tails, shelled (page 56) and chopped

8 lettuce leaves

8 chicory leaves (Belgian endive)

2 sprigs of fresh parsley, chopped

1 lemon, sliced

Chicory adds an almost piquant flavour to this traditional recipe. Once known as succory, chicory (Cichorium intybus) is a tall plant that grows well in Ireland. The leaves and roots have a slightly bitter quality and are used in salads and as a vegetable.

Place the cream in a bowl and mix in the vinegar, horseradish, tomato purée, Worcestershire sauce, Tabasco sauce, and salt and pepper to taste to make a sauce. Stir in the prawns. Line four bowls with the lettuce and chicory leaves, then spoon in the prawn mixture and garnish with the parsley and lemon slices.

DUBLIN LAWYER

If you buy a live lobster, cover the tail with a cloth and hold it firmly on a board. Insert a sharp knife into the cross at the centre of the head and press through to the board. The lobster will be killed instantly. Cook the lobster in boiling water until it turns pink. Once cooled, place back-upwards on a board and cut lengthways through both body and head. Twist off the legs and claws. Remove and discard the head sac and the dark thread from the body and tail. Remove the meat from the body as well as the green liver and the red coral roe in the female. Reserve and clean the half shells. Crack the claws with a hammer and remove the meat using a skewer. Cut all the meat into chunks.

Heat the butter until foaming in a heavy-based pan. Add the lobster meat to the pan and cook lightly for about 4 minutes. Warm the whiskey, pour over the pan and ignite, then leave until the flames die down. Pour in the cream and heat through gently for a few minutes, without allowing the sauce to boil. Spoon the meat into the half shells and pour over the sauce. Season with salt and pepper and serve hot.

1 fresh lobster, about 1.25 kg/2½ lb in weight

75 g/3 oz/⅓ cup butter

4 tablespoons Irish whiskey

250 ml/8 fl oz/1 cup single (light) cream

¼ teaspoon salt

¼ teaspoon freshly ground black pepper

POTTED IRISH CRAB

900 g/2 lb cooked crab

1 teaspoon lemon juice

¼ teaspoon allspice

¼ teaspoon cayenne

¼ teaspoon salt

¼ teaspoon freshly ground black pepper

225 g/8 oz/1 cup unsalted (sweet) butter

2 tablespoons clarified butter

Another traditional way to serve crab is in its shell. Wash the shell thoroughly, then take a cloth and break the bottom parts of the shell away, where it is clearly defined, leaving a small rim around the underside of the main shell. The meat can then be placed in the shells in bars of brown and white meat. Some cooks also add stripes of chopped, boiled egg whites, and the brown meat mashed together with pepper, salt, mustard and the cooked yolks. Finely chopped parsley is generally used to garnish a dressed crab. Irish shrimps are also potted in butter with a pinch of nutmeg and a drop or two of anchovy essence.

Lay the crab on its back on a board and twist off the claws and legs. Putting the pressure of two thumbs behind and under the body of the crab between its top shell and hard tail parts, lever the body from the shell. Discard the 'dead men's fingers' from the side of the body, the stomach sac in the top of the shell, and any green or spongy substance left in the shell. Scoop out the meat remaining in the shell, keeping the white and brown-coloured meat separate, then cut the body in two and extract any remaining meat with a skewer. Press on the small mouth-part of the crab's body and this should snap away. Crack the claws and legs and scoop out the meat from the sides of the shell.

Preheat the oven to 180°C/350°F/gas mark 4. Season both types of meat with the lemon juice, allspice, cayenne, salt and pepper. Spoon the meat in alternate layers into ramekin dishes. Melt the butter, then pour it gently over the meat in the ramekins, letting it soak into the meat. Stand the ramekin dishes in a roasting tin and fill with boiling water to come half way up the sides of the dishes. Bake in the oven for 25 minutes, then remove from the bain-marie and leave to cool. Pour over the clarified butter to seal the top. Serve with brown bread and butter.

Fish

Although the Emerald Isle is surrounded by seas teeming with fish and other edible seafood, fish recipes are few and far between; until recently, the Irish have generally preferred meat and vegetable dishes to fish meals, even during the Great Potato Famine in the mid-nineteenth century. However, Ireland does have a long tradition of fishing, and today there are a number of significant fishing ports, including Ardglass, Kilkeel and Portavogie.

The traditional fishing vessel unique to the west coast of Ireland is the currach, which dates back thousands of years. These high-prowed boats are shaped like a large canoe and are made from a wooden frame covered with tarred cloth. They are still made to the traditional design in the sleepy little fishing village of Ballydavid in County Kerry. In some places, the rounded coracle – constructed in a similar way – is still in use, mainly for fishing on rivers or lakes.

You will find fish served as you travel around the island, however, and they will often be called by their

Fresh ling we'll have and
mackerel, with lobster,
crab and wrasse;
The turbot too will be there,
the gurnet and the bass.
And noble though the pike
is, arrayed upon a dish,
In splendour none can rival
the salmon, prince of fish.

———

from *The Blind Bard of the West*
by Anthony Raferty (1784–1835)

Gaelic names. It is always nice to know a few local words when travelling in a foreign country and it is especially useful to have some of these names to hand when eating fish in the more remote parts of Ireland – although you may still find the pronunciation difficult. In Irish, the common cod is known as *trosc*, and codling, or small cod, are often used as they are common in Irish waters. Because they are so versatile, you can find them cooked in all sorts of ways – baked, fried, grilled, poached or steamed – and they are at their best from May until October.

Flounder, the tasty flat fish, is known as fluke in Ireland and is commonly caught in the shallows and rock pools of the west. Plaice are known as *leathog*, and the brill is *broit*. *Crudan* is gunard, while wrasse are known as *ballach*, both conger eel and the common eel are called *eascu*, and ling goes by the name of *longa*. In Gaelic, the whiting is *faoitin*, and in Northern Ireland, the scad is known as crake herring. The oily mackerel, or *ronnach*, is at its best between October and March and can often be found on Irish menus either grilled, fried, baked or steamed.

Haddock are locally known as *cadog*, and at one time, the haddock caught in Dublin Bay were as famous and sought after as its prawns. Salting tends to ruin the delicate flavour of the haddock, so the Irish preserved them by drying and smoking. In some places, haddock was traditionally sun-dried. An old Irish remedy for toothache goes back to the loaves and fishes of Biblical times. It is said that to carry two haddock jawbones in your pocket is a potent preventative against toothache; the older the bones, the more powerful the magic.

From the Middle Ages until the late 1700s, Ireland exported vast quantities of salted fish to the Continent. These were mainly herrings, *cadan*, cod from Munster and Connaught, and salmon, *bradan*, salted and exported from a large fishery in Galway. The fish were gutted, then packed in barrels according to their size and quality.

Salmon trout, sea trout and brown trout are commonly called *breac geal*, and a variety of traditional salmon and trout dishes can be tasted at the Limerick Food Festival in June, the Kinsale International Gourmet Festival in October, or the Ballina Salmon Festival. As the quote from Anthony Raferty on page 63 suggests, salmon has always been highly regarded in Irish cuisine and smoked salmon is a particular specialty. There are more than 20 major producers of smoked wild and farmed salmon and trout in Ireland, and most use the traditional peat or oak smoking methods. Some, such as Arran Salmon, offer such delicacies as salmon smoked with truffles or wild garlic.

IRISH TROSC BAKE

SERVES
4

450 g/1 lb potatoes, thinly sliced

450 g/1 lb cod fillet, skinned and cubed

1 onion, grated

50 g/2 oz mushrooms, sliced

¼ teaspoon salt

¼ teaspoon freshly ground black pepper

275 g/10 oz/1 medium can of tomato soup

1 tablespoon finely chopped fresh parsley

Trosc is the Gaelic for cod, but you can use any similar white fish for this tasty recipe.

Preheat the oven to 200°C/400°F/gas mark 6. Cook the potatoes in boiling salted water until tender, then drain. Lay the fish in a greased baking dish, top with onion, mushrooms and a layer of potato slices. Season with salt and pepper. Pour the soup over the potatoes. Bake in the oven for about 25 minutes until cooked through and bubbling hot. Serve sprinkled with the parsley.

COCKLED CODLING

This dish is flavoured with the slightly aniseed fennel (Foeniculum vulgare), a perennial herb related to dill, which is commonly used in Irish cooking with fish, lamb, chicken, egg and cheese dishes. Irish Benedictine monks favoured the use of fennel, but its history as a magical herb goes back to pagan times when it was used to work spells, protect against curses and to invoke spirits.

Preheat the oven to 200°C/400°F/gas mark 6. Place the onion slices in a saucepan, cover with water and bring to the boil. Simmer for about 3 minutes until softened, then drain. Cook the potatoes in boiling water until tender, then drain and halve. Arrange the fish in a baking dish and sprinkle with the fennel, thyme, salt and pepper. Place the cockles in a large saucepan, cover with water and bring to the boil. Boil until the shells open, discarding any that remain closed. Lift the cockles from the liquid, remove them from their shells and add them to the fish. Strain the juice from the cockle pan over the fish. Arrange the onions and potatoes around the fish, then spoon over the melted butter. Bake in the oven for 15 minutes, basting occasionally, until cooked through and bubbling hot. Serve sprinkled with parsley and garnish with lemon slices.

3 small onions, sliced

6 potatoes

700 g/1½ lb codling fillets

1 tablespoon finely chopped fennel

½ teaspoon finely chopped fresh thyme

a pinch of salt

a pinch of freshly ground black pepper

24 cockles, cleaned

25 g/1 oz/2 tablespoons butter, melted

1 tablespoon finely chopped fresh parsley

½ lemon, sliced

SERVES

4

HADDOCK IN CIDER

6 haddock fillets, skinned

450 ml/¾ pint/2 cups dry cider

¼ teaspoon salt

¼ teaspoon freshly ground
black pepper

50 g/2 oz/¼ cup butter

100 g/4 oz mushrooms, sliced

½ tablespoon plain (all-purpose)
flour

1 tablespoon milk

2 teaspoons chopped fresh dill
(dillweed)

Lay the fillets in a flameproof baking dish, pour over the cider and season with salt and pepper. Bring to a simmer, then cover and poach gently for about 10 minutes until the fish is cooked. Melt half the butter in a separate pan and sauté the mushrooms until soft, then remove the mushrooms from the pan and keep them warm. Add the rest of butter to the pan, then stir in the flour and milk to make a paste. Remove the fish from the heat and strain off the cooking liquor into the second pan. Whisk together to make a sauce, mix in the dill and cook for 2 minutes, stirring. Arrange the mushrooms over the fish, then pour on the sauce. Brown under a hot grill until golden and bubbling.

CODDLED MONKFISH

Preheat the oven to 180°C/350°F/gas mark 4. Combine the sauce ingredients into a paste. Place one fillet in the bottom of a greased baking dish. Smear the paste over the fillet and place the other fillet on top. Pour the milk around the fish and arrange onion slices on top. Cover with baking foil and bake in the oven for 30 minutes. Meanwhile, mix the butter and egg yolk into the mashed potatoes, then beat the egg white until stiff and fold it into the potatoes. Remove the fish from the oven and cover with potato mix. Bake for a further 15 minutes until the top is lightly browned. Serve garnished with the parsley and lemon wedges.

2 x 175 g/6 oz monkfish fillets

250 ml/8 fl oz/1 cup milk

1 onion, sliced

1 tablespoon butter

1 egg, separated

450 g/1 lb mashed potatoes

4 sprigs of fresh parsley

2 lemons, cut into wedges

For the sauce

3 tablespoons brown breadcrumbs

25 g/1 oz/2 tablespoons butter, melted

2 teaspoons lemon juice

1 tablespoon finely chopped fresh parsley

½ teaspoon dried tarragon

½ teaspoon dried dill (dillweed)

salt and freshly ground black pepper

SERVES

4

TARRAGON FLUKE

4 flounder fillets

2 tablespoons finely chopped tarragon leaves

2 tablespoons lemon juice

1 garlic clove, crushed

75 g/3 oz/⅓ cup butter

1 tablespoon plain (all-purpose) flour

¼ teaspoon salt

¼ teaspoon freshly ground black pepper

1 teaspoon vegetable oil

If you cannot buy flounder, you can substitute another flat fish. Tarragon (Artemisia dracunculus) *is a strongly flavoured perennial European herb used sparingly in sauces and vegetable dishes. Tarragon vinegar, a favourite fish accompaniment, can be made by steeping the leaves in wine vinegar.*

Place the fish in a glass or ceramic bowl. Mix half the tarragon with the lemon juice and garlic, sprinkle over the fish and leave to marinate for 30 minutes. Heat half the butter in a frying pan until the foam subsides. Season the flour with salt and pepper. Lift the fish from the marinade and coat in the seasoned flour. Turn the fish in the hot butter until coated, then cook for about 5 minutes until cooked through. Mix the remaining tarragon leaves with the remaining butter and the oil and shape into two butter pats. Place the cooked fish on a serving plate and top with the tarragon butter.

CADOG COBBLER

Preheat the oven to 200°C/400°F/gas mark 6. To make the sauce, heat the béchamel sauce to below boiling. Mix the mustard to a paste with the milk, then stir it into the sauce with the cheese and heat very gently until blended. Set aside. Arrange the fish in a greased baking dish and pour the cheese sauce over the fish. Mix together the flour, baking powder and salt, then rub in the butter and stir in half the cheese. Mix to a dough with the egg yolk and milk. Roll out on a lightly floured board and cut into 5 cm (2 inch) rounds with a pastry cutter. Arrange the scones over the fish and brush the tops with milk. Sprinkle the rest of the cheese over the top. Bake in the oven for about 30 minutes until the fish is cooked through and the scone topping is golden brown.

700 g/1½ lb haddock fillets, skinned and cut into chunks

225 g/8 oz/2 cups plain (all-purpose) flour

1 teaspoon baking powder

a pinch of salt

50 g/2 oz/¼ cup butter

75 g/3 oz/¾ cup medium Irish cheese, grated

1 egg yolk

3 tablespoons milk

For the sauce

600 ml/1 pint/2½ cups Béchamel Sauce (page 80)

½ teaspoon mustard powder

2 teaspoons milk

175 g/6 oz/1½ cups hard Irish cheese, finely grated

STUFFED LEATHOG

SERVES

4

2 x 350 g/12 oz plaice fillets

1 onion, sliced

250 ml/8 fl oz/1 cup milk

1 tablespoon butter

1 egg, separated

6 potatoes, boiled and mashed

1 tablespoon chopped fresh parsley

**300 ml/½ pint/1¼ cups
Parsley Sauce (page 82)**

For the stuffing

3 tablespoons fresh breadcrumbs

25 g/1 oz/2 tablespoons butter

½ teaspoon dried mixed herbs

**¼ teaspoon freshly ground
black pepper**

Preheat the oven to 200°C/400°F/gas mark 6. Place one fish fillet skin-side down in a greased baking dish. Mix together the stuffing ingredients and spread over the fillet. Lay the second fillet skin-side up on the top. Spread the onion slices over the top, then pour in the milk. Cover with greaseproof paper and cook in the oven for 30 minutes. Mash the butter and egg yolk into the potatoes. Fold in the egg white, and spread the mixture over the fish. Return to the oven for about 15 minutes until golden brown. Garnish with parsley and serve with parsley sauce.

TIPSY CADAN

This interesting dish of herring cooked in stout is flavoured with thyme. A pungent aromatic herb, thyme (Thymus vulgaris) has a number of uses and is used in Irish cooking to flavour anything from chicken and veal to vegetables, fish and game. This ancient herb is also therapeutic, with antiseptic and antibiotic qualities.

Preheat the oven to 190°C/375°F/gas mark 5. Mix the carrots, chopped onions, garlic, herbs and spices in a saucepan. Pour in the stout and bring to the boil, then simmer for about 10 minutes until the vegetables are cooked. Turn out into a large baking dish, arrange the herrings on top and cover with onion rings. Pour in the light ale and vinegar and season with salt and pepper. Bake in the oven for 20 minutes until the fish is cooked through. Leave to cool, then serve with Irish soda bread.

2 carrots, sliced

2 onions, chopped

1 garlic clove, finely chopped

2 teaspoons finely chopped
fresh parsley

¼ teaspoon dried thyme

1 bay leaf

4 peppercorns

3 cloves

600 ml/1 pint/2½ cups Irish stout

10 small herrings

1 onion, sliced into rings

300 ml/½ pint/1¼ cups light ale

1 tablespoon vinegar

salt and freshly ground black pepper

RONNACH
IN GOOSEBERRY SAUCE

SERVES

4

50 g/2 oz/¼ cup butter, melted

1 large onion, finely chopped

450 g/1 lb gooseberries, halved

salt and freshly ground black pepper

2 tablespoons fresh breadcrumbs

4 x 450 g/1 lb mackerel fillets

½ teaspoon finely chopped fresh
fennel fronds

2 tablespoons caster
(superfine) sugar

2 tablespoons water

½ teaspoon grated lemon rind

Preheat the oven to 200°C/400°F/gas mark 6. Melt the butter in a small saucepan and sauté the onion for about 5 minutes until soft. Add half the gooseberries, season with salt and pepper, and cook for 5 minutes. Remove from the heat and stir in the breadcrumbs. Spread the paste on the flat mackerel fillets, sprinkle with fennel, then roll them up. Place them on a greased baking dish and bake in the oven for 20 minutes. Place the remaining gooseberries in a saucepan with the sugar, water and lemon rind, bring to the boil, then simmer for about 10 minutes until soft. Purée in a blender. Serve the rolled fillets with the sauce poured over.

VIKING SALMON

In this dish, the salt and herb mixture actually 'cooks' the flesh of the fish, and this was a simple way for people to preserve fish before refrigeration. The flavouring herb is dill (Anethum graveolens), *which has pungently aromatic, feathery leaves, similar to anise in quality, which go well with fish dishes as well as in pickles. The aromatic seeds are also used in Irish cooking. An infusion of the leaves used to be used to soothe the stomach and stimulate the system.*

Clean the salmon, slice in half lengthways and de-bone. Place one salmon piece skin-side down in a casserole dish and sprinkle with the dill. Mix together the sugar, salt, and peppercorns and sprinkle over the dill. Place the second salmon piece skin-side up on top. Place a large plate on the top of the salmon and place some heavy weights on the plate to weigh the salmon down. Put the dish in a refrigerator for 12 hours. Remove from the refrigerator, turn the salmon over, and replace the plate and weights. Replace in the refrigerator for a further 12 hours. Repeat this three more times over a three-day period. Once the fish is marinated, scrape off the salt-dill mixture and pat the fish dry on kitchen paper. Slice very thinly and serve with mustard sauce.

1.5 kg/3 lb salmon

3 tablespoons chopped fresh dill (dillweed)

1½ tablespoons caster (superfine) sugar

4 tablespoons salt

2 tablespoons white peppercorns, crushed

FLUTHERED WILD SALMON

SERVES

4

1 x 1.5 kg/3 lb tail of wild salmon

5 tablespoons sea salt

3 tablespoons Irish whiskey

2 tablespoons freshly ground black pepper

2 tablespoons soft brown sugar

1 tablespoon lemon juice

2 tablespoons finely chopped fresh thyme

2 teaspoons finely chopped fresh dill (dillweed)

'Fluthered', in local Dublin slang, means drunk, and the following recipe for marinating wild salmon includes a few generous nips of Irish whiskey. This recipe, an Irish form of gravlax, is made with pure, coarse-grained sea salt, made by purifying sea water, then evaporating off the water.

Scale, de-fin, and bone the fish, and divide it into two fillets. Mix together the salt, whiskey, pepper, sugar and lemon juice. Sprinkle the thyme and dill in the bottom of a large baking dish, spoon over 3 tablespoons of the whiskey mixture and place one salmon fillet skin-side down on the top. Spoon almost all the rest of the whiskey mixture over the salmon flesh and place the other fillet skin-side up on the top, finishing with the remaining mixture. Cover with baking foil and place a heavy weight on the fish. Leave in a cool place for three days for the marinade to permeate the fish. Remove the fish from the marinade and clean off the marinade. Serve very thinly sliced.

SPINACH-DRESSED SALMON

SERVES

4

Divide the lettuce between four plates and arrange two salmon slices on each one. Purée the spinach, oil, vinegar and lemon juice together, then season with salt and pepper. Pour the dressing over the salmon and lettuce and serve.

4 lettuce leaves, shredded
8 slices of smoked salmon

For the dressing
50 g/2 oz baby spinach leaves
120 ml/4 fl oz/½ cup vegetable oil
1½ tablespoons balsamic vinegar
½ teaspoon lemon juice
salt and freshly ground black pepper

COUNTRY HERB TROUT

SERVES

4

1 lemon

2 sprigs of fresh tarragon

2 sprigs of fresh thyme

4 fresh trout

50 g/2 oz/¼ cup butter

1 tablespoon flaked
(slivered) almonds

1 small onion, thinly sliced
into rings

½ green (bell) pepper, seeded and
sliced into thin rings

1 tablespoon tarragon wine vinegar

3 tablespoons plain yoghurt

1 hard-boiled (hard-cooked) egg,
finely chopped

salt and freshly ground black pepper

4 sprigs of fresh parsley

Squeeze the juice from half the lemon and cut the second piece in half. Place a tarragon sprig, a thyme sprig and a lemon quarter in each trout cavity. Place a piece of greased baking foil on a grill tray and place fish on the foil. Dot with about one-quarter of the butter and cook under a hot grill for 5 minutes. Turn the fish over, dot with one-third of the remaining butter and cook for a further 5 minutes. Toss the almonds in half the remaining butter, then brown them quickly under the grill. Heat the remaining butter in a small pan and sauté the onion and pepper rings for a few minutes until soft. Mix in the vinegar and yoghurt. Stir in the egg, season with salt and pepper and heat through gently. Place the fish on plates and pour over the lemon juice. Spoon the sauce beside each fish and decorate with the sprigs of parsley.

SAUCES FOR FISH

Most of the following sauces are traditionally served hot with poached, baked or steamed firm, white fish, although tartare sauce is made a different way and is served cold. Although there are traditional combinations of seafood and sauce, the final choice of which fish or seafood is best served with which sauce is a matter of personal taste. Many of these sauces are based on the classic béchamel sauce, which was said to have been invented in France in the late seventeenth century, when Louis de Béchamel, Marquis de Nointel and a steward in the household of King Louis XIV, introduced it to the royal table for the first time.

BÉCHAMEL SAUCE

MAKES

600 ml/1 pint/2½ cups

1 small onion

4 cloves

600 ml/1 pint/2½ cups milk

6 peppercorns

1 bay leaf

50 g/2 oz/¼ cup butter, unsalted

50 g/2 oz/½ cup plain
(all-purpose) flour

Stud the onion with the cloves and place in a saucepan with the milk, peppercorns and bay leaf. Bring to the boil, then remove from the heat and leave to stand for 30 minutes. Strain the flavoured milk into a bowl. Melt the butter in a clean saucepan until foaming, then stir in the flour to create a paste and cook for 1 minute, stirring continuously. Remove from the heat and whisk in the milk, then return to the heat and heat gently until the sauce thickens, stirring all the time until the mixture is smooth. Rub through a sieve, if necessary, to eliminate any lumps.

EGG SAUCE

Remove the yolks from the hard-boiled eggs and use for another recipe. Heat the sauce gently to just below boiling, then remove from the heat. Press the egg whites through a sieve into the sauce, season with salt and pepper, stir well and heat through gently.

**600 ml/1 pint/2½ cups Béchamel
Sauce (page 80)**

3 hard-boiled (hard-cooked) eggs

¼ teaspoon salt

**¼ teaspoon freshly ground
black pepper**

PARSLEY SAUCE

MAKES
600 ml/1 pint/2½ cups

2 tablespoons finely chopped fresh parsley

600 ml/1 pint/2½ cups Béchamel Sauce (page 80)

Parsley (Petroselinum crispum) *is among the most common herbs in many national cuisines and Ireland is no exception. It can be used both for flavouring and for garnish, and parsley sauce is particularly good with fish. The Irish used to make parsley tea, which was a good source of iron and therefore occasionally drunk as a tonic as well as a remedy for rheumatism.*

Add the parsley to the sauce and heat through gently.

BÉCHAMEL
AND MUSTARD SAUCE

———

Mix together the mustard and vinegar to a paste, then mix this into the sauce with the lemon juice and chilli. Bring to the boil, then remove the chilli. Reduce the heat and stir in the egg yolks and cream. Heat the sauce to just below boiling, then serve.

½ teaspoon mustard powder

1 tablespoon malt vinegar

600 ml/1 pint/2½ cups Béchamel Sauce (page 80)

½ teaspoon lemon juice

1 small fresh chilli

2 egg yolks

175 ml/6 fl oz/¾ cup double (heavy) cream

HERRING ROE SAUCE

600 ml/1 pint/2½ cups

50 g/2 oz/¼ cup butter

225 g/8 oz soft herring roes

600 ml/1 pint/2½ cups Béchamel Sauce (page 80)

½ tablespoon mustard

1 teaspoon lemon juice

Melt half the butter in a small saucepan and cook the roes over a low heat for about 5 minutes until soft. Warm the sauce, then rub the roes through a sieve into the sauce. Stir in the mustard and lemon juice, then add the remaining butter and let it melt into the sauce over a low heat.

T A R T A R E   S A U C E

MAKES
300 ml/½ pint/1¼ cups

Tartare sauce is a classic accompaniment for seafood, especially delicately flavoured fish like plaice.

Whisk together the egg yolk and vinegar, then gradually pour on the oil a drop at a time, whisking continuously until the sauce thickens and emulsifies. Remove the yolks from the hard-boiled eggs and rub them through a sieve into the sauce. Rub one egg white through a sieve into the sauce, then stir in the capers, parsley and chives and season with salt and pepper.

1 egg yolk

1 tablespoon wine vinegar

300 ml/½ pint/1¼ cups corn oil

2 hard-boiled (hard-cooked) eggs

1 teaspoon capers, chopped

**1 teaspoon finely chopped
fresh parsley**

1 teaspoon chopped fresh chives

salt and freshly ground black pepper

Potatoes

Potatoes were first cultivated thousands of miles from Ireland. An indigenous product of South America, they were grown – many thousands of years before the arrival of Europeans – by the ancient Incas, who lived in the high Andes mountains. They used to preserve them in the frosty nights and the hot tropical sun by freeze-drying them into a form called *chuno*. The cold climate and damp atmosphere of their original home around Lake Titicaca was ideally matched to that of Ireland, which is why potatoes took so well to the Irish conditions. For some reason, the early Spanish naturalists who first came across the potato cross-pollinated its name with that of the Caribbean sweet potato, or *batatas*, hence the word 'potato'.

Some historians suggest that it was the naval admiral and first slave-trader Sir John Hawkins who first introduced the potato to England in 1563. It was reputedly Sir Walter Raleigh who first brought them to Ireland from his colony in Virginia, USA, in the 1580s. Raleigh was

Do not be down-hearted, but cheer up once more,
The provision is coming from each foreign shore,
Good beer, flour and butter, rich sugar and tea,
From Russia and Prussia and Amerikay.

———

Old Irish rhyme

appointed Mayor of Youghal in County Cork until he fell out of favour with Queen Elizabeth I. On her death in 1603, he was imprisoned in the Tower of London by King James I, and beheaded by the axe, which he ruefully called 'a sharp medicine, but an infallible cure!'.

Sir Walter Raleigh met the famous poet Edmund Spenser (1552–99) at Castle Matrix in County Limerick in 1580, and presented him with his New World tubers. Spenser went on to cultivate the first potatoes in Ireland. Raleigh also gave some potatoes to Lord Southwell, who became the first person to devise the open-field method of cultivation in Ireland. The annual Walter Raleigh Potato Festival is still held in Youghal.

In the seventeenth and eighteenth centuries, the potato became the staple diet in Ireland, as under British rule the wealth of Irish dairy produce and cereals were reserved for export to England. Also, potatoes were easy to grow in Ireland's rich soil and therefore soon dominated the local vegetable plots. In the early days, potatoes were cooked in a special, usually three-legged, iron pot over a turf fire, and they were then drained in a wicker basket. In England, on the other hand, it took the bad northern European grain harvests of the late seventeenth and eighteenth centuries to force people to accept the potato as a regular part of the diet.

Even as early as the first famines of the early 1740s, Edmund Burke wrote, 'Whoever travels through this kingdom will see such poverty as few nations in Europe can equal.' By the early nineteenth century, half of Ireland's peasantry had forsaken traditional cultivation. The forced subdivision of a farmer's smallholding amongst his surviving sons under the conacre system meant that a living had to be eked out from less than an acre of land. As the potato thrived throughout the island, even those areas with poor soil, it was rapidly adopted as the crop of choice. Indeed, many poor people ate nothing else. By 1845, the rapidly growing Irish population numbered eight million people. When a blight struck the potato crops for three years in a row, therefore, the results were disastrous. During the Great Famine of 1845–7, millions of Irish people emigrated to North America to escape starvation, while over 250,000 people died in 1847 alone.

There are several hundred varieties of potatoes grown throughout the world, and the white Irish variety of potatoes known as *Solanum tuberosum* are said to be among the sweetest and fluffiest anywhere. Arguably the best new potatoes in Ireland are the Comer variety from County Down. The versatility of the potato, whether new or old, gave rise to a wealth of imaginative ways of cooking with potatoes. With protein, vitamins, minerals and fibre, little fat or salt and plenty of easily assimilated starch, they are among the most nutritious of foods.

IRISH CHAMP

300 ml/½ pint/1¼ cups milk

100 g/4 oz spring onions
(scallions), chopped

8 potatoes, boiled and mashed

100 g/4 oz/½ cup butter

¼ teaspoon salt

¼ teaspoon freshly ground
black pepper

Champ, also known in some localities as stelk, *is a classic Irish potato dish and can be made in a communal casserole dish or in individual bowls. It is very similar to Colcannon (page 119) and is a version of the traditional* coiblide, *in which onions replace the spring onions. Chives or shallots are often substituted for spring onions, and parsley is sometimes added to basic champ. Other recipes include carrots pre-cooked in milk, peas and even nettles. A spoon is used to take the champ from the outside of the dish and dip it in the melted butter in the centre before eating.*

Bring the milk to the boil with the spring onions, then simmer for about 5 minutes until tender. Mix the milk and spring onions into the mashed potato. Spoon the mixture into eight ramekin dishes. Make an indentation in the centre of each dish of potato. Cut the butter into eight pieces and place one in each of the hollows. Sprinkle a little salt and pepper on each dish and serve.

IRISH POTATO CAKES

SERVES
4

450 g/1 lb potatoes
65 g/2½ oz/⅓ cup salted butter
1 teaspoon salt
½ teaspoon freshly ground black pepper
3 tablespoons plain (all-purpose) flour

Place the potatoes in a saucepan, cover with water, bring to the boil and simmer for about 15 minutes until tender. Drain, then mash with half the butter, the salt and pepper and mix in the flour. Turn the mixture out on to a floured board and roll out to about 2 cm (¾ inch) thick. Cut into 7.5 cm (3 inch) rounds with a knife or biscuit cutter. Melt the remaining butter in a large frying pan and sauté the potato cakes for about 10 minutes until golden on both sides. Drain and serve hot.

CELTIC PANCAKES

Cook the potatoes in boiling water for about 15 minutes until soft, then drain. Rub the cooked potatoes through a sieve, then leave to cool. Mix the butter into the potatoes, then stir in the egg, flour and salt. Mix the bicarbonate of soda into the buttermilk, then stir this into the potato mix. Butter a hot griddle or heavy-based frying pan. Drop tablespoons of the mixture on to the griddle and brown the pancakes for a few minutes on each side, repeating until you have used all the mixture.

SERVES

4

3 potatoes

25 g/1 oz/2 tablespoons butter, melted

1 egg, beaten

3 tablespoons plain (all-purpose) flour

1 teaspoon salt

1 teaspoon bicarbonate of soda (baking soda)

4 tablespoons buttermilk

SERVES

4

450 g/1 lb potatoes

75 g/3 oz/⅓ cup butter

2 teaspoons salt

**100 g/4 oz/1 cup plain
(all-purpose) flour**

COTTAGE POTATO SCONES

Cook the potatoes in boiling water for about 15 minutes until soft. Drain well, then mash with half the butter and the salt. Work the flour into the potato mash until stiff. Turn out on to a floured board and shape into 12 equal pieces. Roll the pieces into balls and flatten slightly. Heat the remaining butter and sauté the scones for about 5 minutes on each side until browned, then serve hot with butter.

FARMER'S POTATOES

Preheat the oven to 180°C/350°F/gas mark 4. Cook the potatoes in boiling water for 5–10 minutes until just soft, then drain. Arrange half the potato slices on the bottom of a greased baking dish. Melt the butter and sauté the bacon and onion until soft, then add the pepper. Spoon the bacon and onion mixture over the potatoes. Arrange the rest of the potatoes over the bacon and onion. Mix the cream and milk, then pour this over the top and cover with cheese slices. Dot the shallot slices on top of the cheese. Bake in the oven for about 30 minutes until cooked through and golden on top.

700 g/1½ lb potatoes, sliced

1 tablespoon butter

175 g/6 oz streaky bacon, rinded and diced

1 small onion, thinly sliced

½ teaspoon freshly ground black pepper

150 ml/¼ pint/⅔ cup single (light) cream

3 tablespoons milk

100 g/4 oz/1 cup hard Irish cheese, sliced

1 shallot, thinly sliced

SERVES

4

O'BRIEN'S POTATOES

———

4 potatoes

1 leek, boiled and sliced

2 onions, finely chopped

2 tablespoons plain (all-purpose) flour

a pinch of salt

6 tablespoons hot milk

100 g/4 oz/1 cup mature Irish cheese, grated

50 g/2 oz/1 cup dry brown breadcrumbs

50 g/2 oz/¼ cup butter

a pinch of cayenne

Preheat the oven to 180°C/350°F/gas mark 4. Cook the potatoes in boiling water for about 15 minutes, then drain and slice. Mix the potatoes with the leek, onion, flour and salt, then stir in the milk and three-quarters of the cheese. Grease a baking dish and pour in the mixture. Sprinkle the mixture with breadcrumbs, then the remaining cheese. Dot pieces of the butter over the dish and sprinkle with cayenne. Cook in the oven for about 35 minutes until the top browns and bubbles, then serve piping hot.

SAFFRON POTATOES

———

Saffron was first brought to England by a pilgrim in the mid-1300s during the reign of Edward III and was grown in Saffron Walden in Essex, giving the town its name, as well as Cambridge and Cornwall. It has always been the most expensive spice, since it is made from the dried stamens of the saffron crocus (Crocus sativus) *all of which must be picked by hand. It takes around 30,000 stamens to produce 225 g/8 oz of saffron. When first grown in England, it was such an important commodity that any adulteration of the crop was punishable by death. After a while, its importance declined in most of England, except in Cornwall, and it was probably from Cornwall that saffron came to Ireland in the days of King Mark, who was betrothed to Isolde, the daughter of an Irish king. Highly aromatic with a distinctive orange-red colouring, saffron is used particularly in rice dishes such as paella.*

900 g/2 lb potatoes

¼ teaspoon salt

450 g/1 lb hard Irish cheese, grated

¼ teaspoon freshly ground black pepper

3 saffron strands

4 tablespoons lamb or chicken stock

4 tablespoons single (light) cream

40 g/1½ oz/3 tablespoons butter

Preheat the oven to 180°C/350°F/gas mark 4. Cook the potatoes in boiling salted water for about 15 minutes until tender, then drain, cool and slice thinly. Arrange a layer of slices in a greased baking dish, cover with a little cheese and a sprinkling of pepper, then repeat until all the potatoes are used, reserving a tablespoon of the cheese. Soak the saffron in a little boiling water, then mix with the stock, cream and remaining cheese. Pour the mixture over the potatoes and dot with the butter. Bake in the oven for 20 minutes until golden brown on top.

APPLE AND POTATO SALAD

———

Cook the potatoes in boiling water with 2 sprigs of mint for about 15 minutes until tender. Drain, then quarter. Slice the apple into segments and sprinkle with lemon juice. Make a mayonnaise by beating together the mustard and egg yolk. Gradually whisk in the oil a drop at a time until the mixture emulsifies and thickens. Stir in the cider and chopped mint and season with salt and pepper. Toss the apple and potatoes in the mayonnaise. Chill, then serve garnished with the remaining mint sprigs.

450 g/1 lb new potatoes

4 generous sprigs of fresh mint

1 green eating (dessert) apple, peeled and cored

1 tablespoon lemon juice

1 teaspoon mustard

1 egg yolk

150 ml/¼ pint/⅔ cup vegetable oil

1 tablespoon dry cider

1 tablespoon chopped fresh mint leaves

¼ teaspoon salt

¼ teaspoon freshly ground black pepper

Dairy Products

BUTTER AND CREAM

Ireland has always been famous for its rich and creamy butter, as the lush pastures support large herds of productive dairy cattle. The Gaelic word for the greenest grass, watered by a stream, is *glasghaibhlinn* and this pasture produces the best milk, of which the last and richest part is *sniugadh*. In the past, farmers used to make their own produce, but now there are numerous large butteries spread across the country, and some are now diversifying into different dairy products, such as butters flavoured with garlic and herbs or other ingredients. Ireland is now the fourteenth largest producer of butter in the world and much of its produce is exported to other countries. Butter, cream and other dairy products have always been used extensively in Irish cooking.

There are two main types of butter. Sweet cream butter is made from fresh cream, while lactic butter is made from ripened cream to which bacterial agents have been added to improve the flavour. This is salted butter. The cream from around ten litres/18 pints of milk goes

Bachelor's fare; bread and cheese, and kisses.

Jonathan Swift

into making just 450 g/1 lb of butter. With a high energy content, butter contains calcium and vitamins A and D. In medieval times, butter was packed into wooden churns and stored in peat bogs. This bog butter, as it was known, has been found in bogs after hundreds of years. It was sadly inedible, but still smelled like and resembled very cold, hard butter.

Buttermilk, locally known as 'bonny clobber', is used extensively in Irish cooking. Although it is now manufactured using a culture, it was traditionally the liquid left over after churning the butter, and it has a distinctive sour flavour. Once quite difficult to buy in the supermarkets, it is again much more readily available, but you can substitute milk mixed with a teaspoon of lemon juice if necessary. The container generally used to carry buttermilk is known in Gaelic as a *piggin*.

The cream is the part of the milk that contains most of the fat, and the different types of cream have different culinary qualities because of that. Single cream contains 18 per cent butterfat and is used to give a smooth texture and flavour to many dishes, while double cream contains 48 per cent butterfat and is used in richer dishes and for thickening. Another type of cream more usually associated with the West Country of England but also well used in Ireland is clotted cream, and its use probably came over to

Ireland from Cornwall. It is made by leaving milk to stand for 12 hours, then heating it gently and skimming off the crusty layer from the top. In Connaught and Ulster, there are still stories of butter fairies who steal the cream from the top of any milk left standing, and leprechauns who turn the milk sour.

IRISH CHEESE

Cheese, or *cais* in Gaelic, is one of our oldest foods and was probably eaten as long as 11,000 years ago. In Ireland, the art of cheese-making dates back at least to the travelling monks of the ninth and tenth centuries, and cheese has been an important ingredient in the Irish diet since early Christian times. Towards the end of the 1600s, however, the art of making cheese went into something of a decline and by the mid-nineteenth century, around the time of the Great Famine, cheese-making in Ireland had almost died out. Over the past few decades, however, the revival in local cheese-making has produced a wonderful selection of cheeses.

Originally a method of preserving milk, cheese is made by curdling milk with rennet, creating a solid, the curds, and a liquid, the whey. The country way of making an Irish cream cheese was by putting thick curds into a cloth and hanging the cloth bag from the roof of the cottage, letting the thin, watery liquid drain out. The remaining cheese was then placed in a hooped, wooden sieve, pressed down and left to mature. Hard cheeses were made by drawing off the curds, which were then pressed, or moulded, salted, drained, dried, cured and aged, then ripened by various methods to produce the different varieties of cheese, all rich in protein, fat, minerals and vitamin A. The flavour of the final product depends both on exactly how the cheese is made and also on the source of the milk – cows, sheep or goats – and on the pasture on which they have grazed.

About 30 farmhouse cheese-makers currently make over 40 different varieties of traditional Irish cheeses but there are around 170 different Irish cheeses altogether, and they vary considerably in texture and strength from the semi-soft derrynaflan cheese to the hard, unpasteurized gigginstown cheese. Dunlop was originally an Irish cheese which was introduced into Scotland by a refugee from religious persecution in the seventeenth century. It is similar to cheddar but with a moist, fine texture. Also similar to cheddar is Ireland's only raw-milk cheese, made by Baylough in Clogheen, Tipperary. Likened to gouda, coolea cheese is a cows' milk cheese with orange rind which is made in County Cork and is ideal for recipes where grated hard Irish cheese is called for. Another cheese likened to Dutch cheese is ardrahan, also from Cork. The dry and crumbly gabriel cheese is ideal for any recipe that calls for parmesan. Carrigaline Farmhouse produces mild, semi-hard cheeses either natural, or flavoured with garlic and herbs. Friesian cows' milk is used to prepare Riverville Farmhouse cheese in Galway, and three flavours are produced, as well as original: garlic, peppered and spiced.

One of the first Irish blue cheeses to be made in country farmhouses was cashel blue, a cows' milk cheese from Tipperary, which has been compared to gorgonzola.

Mileens, a product of West Cork, is a soft, spicy, creamy cheese with the texture of camembert. The rind of this cheese is washed in salt water as it matures. A similar cheese, made in Thurles in County Tipperary, is Cooleeny Farmhouse cheese, with its white mould rind and gooey inside. The cheeses made at the Carrigbyrne Farmhouse are likened to a cross between camembert and brie. One, musky-flavoured Irish cheese is gubbeen, which is made in Skull in County Cork with vegetarian rennet and unpasteurized cows' milk. These ingredients are also used in durrus cheese, a soft variety with a dark pink rind. Produced in Cork, this is a mellow, wholesome cheese.

Knockanore Farmhouse also makes a variety of cheeses, including oak-smoked, red, garlic, herb, black pepper and chive-flavoured. These cheeses are hand-turned and individually waxed. Oak smoking is also used by Ardrahan Farmhouse, which also produces a semi-soft, rind-washed traditional cheese. Cahills Farm in Limerick flavours its cheeses with red wine, porter, whiskey and fine herbs. Carbery, in County Cork, produces a dubliner cheese, and Compsey, of Tipperary, make a cream cheese. Instantly recognized by their surface designs of the shamrock and Celtic motifs, Dunbarr's soft, cows' milk cheese is produced in Dublin.

The many varieties of Irish cheese also include those made with sheep's or goats' milk. One well known goats' milk cheese is inagh, from Shannon, and Corleggy also makes a mature goats' cheese as well as cows' milk cheeses flavoured with garlic, cumin or green peppercorn, or smoked.

TRADITIONAL IRISH RAREBIT

SERVES

4

Mix together all the ingredients except the bread and paprika in a saucepan. Cook over a low heat, stirring constantly, until the mixture is well blended and hot. Remove from the heat and spread the mixture on the bread slices. Grill under a hot grill for a few minutes until golden brown, then serve sprinkled with a little paprika.

225 g/8 oz/2 cups hard Irish cheese, grated

2 teaspoons cornflour (cornstarch)

1 teaspoon mustard powder

2 teaspoons white vinegar

2 eggs

300 ml/½ pint/1¼ cups milk

a pinch of salt and freshly ground black pepper

a dash of Tabasco sauce

4 slices of Irish wholemeal (wholewheat) bread

¼ teaspoon paprika

TIPSY DUBLIN RAREBIT

SERVES
4

1 tablespoon butter

100 g/4 oz/1 cup hard Irish cheese, finely grated

1 teaspoon mustard powder

2 tablespoons Irish stout

4 thick slices of brown bread

¼ teaspoon cayenne

Melt the butter in a saucepan over a low heat, then add the cheese and very gently allow it to melt. Mix the mustard with a little of the stout, then stir it into the remaining stout. Mix this into the cheese and butter. Toast the bread on both sides. Press down on the centre of the toast slices, creating a flat, well shape. Carefully spoon the stout and cheese mixture over the toast and place under a hot grill for a few minutes until browned. Serve sprinkled with the cayenne.

SORREL SOUFFLÉ

The sorrel used in cooking is garden sorrel (Rumex acetosa), *and in Irish tradition it symbolizes affection. Both the leaves and stem of this perennial herb are used in egg, fish, vegetable or chicken recipes. Sorrel soup is a traditional favourite in Irish country cuisine. This light soufflé can be served as a light meal or as a side dish with fish or chicken.*

Preheat the oven to 180°C/350°F/gas mark 4. Pour the milk over the breadcrumbs and leave to soak. Melt the butter in a large saucepan, add the sorrel and cook gently for about 3 minutes until the sorrel wilts. Beat the egg yolks, then stir them into the sorrel with the milk and breadcrumbs. Sprinkle the cheese over the base of a greased soufflé dish. Beat the egg whites with a pinch of salt and pepper until stiff, then fold them gently into the sorrel mixture. Pour the mixture into the dish and bake in the oven for about 20 minutes until the top has risen and browned slightly. Serve at once.

3 tablespoons milk

3 tablespoons white breadcrumbs

50 g/2 oz/¼ cup butter

450 g/1 lb fresh sorrel, cleaned and chopped

2 eggs, separated

4 tablespoons grated hard cheese

salt and white pepper

SERVES

4

350 g/12 oz potatoes

2 egg yolks, beaten

2 tablespoons double (heavy) cream

40 g/1½ oz/½ cup hard Irish cheese, grated

a pinch of dried basil

a pinch of cayenne

½ teaspoon salt

½ teaspoon black pepper

2 tablespoons plain (all-purpose) flour

1 egg, beaten

3 tablespoons white breadcrumbs

3 tablespoons oil

CHEESE AND POTATO CAKES

Cook the potatoes in boiling water for about 15 minutes until tender, then drain and rub through a sieve. Beat the egg yolks with the cream, then stir into the hot potatoes. Stir in the cheese, basil and cayenne, and season with salt and pepper. Shape the mixture into small cakes. Coat the cakes with flour, then dip them in the beaten egg and coat with breadcrumbs. Heat the oil in a heavy-based frying pan and fry the cakes for about 10 minutes until golden brown on both sides.

CHEESE AND CHIVE SOUFFLÉ

Chives (Allium schoenoprasum) *are a member of the onion family, all of which are used frequently in Irish cooking. As they have a delicate flavour, chives are used particularly in light egg dishes as well as sauces, soups and salads.*

Preheat the oven to 200°C/400°F/gas mark 6. Beat the egg yolks with the Tabasco, salt and pepper, then beat in the cottage cheese a little at a time. Whisk the egg whites until stiff, then fold gently into the mixture with the chives and parsley. Butter a small flameproof baking dish and heat on the hob until hot. Pour in the mixture and turn the heat down very low. Leave on the heat for about 3 minutes, then transfer to a hot oven for about 10 minutes until the soufflé has risen and browned. Serve immediately.

4 eggs, separated

a dash of Tabasco sauce

¼ teaspoon salt

¼ teaspoon white pepper

225 g/8 oz/1 cup cottage cheese

2 tablespoons finely chopped fresh chives

1 tablespoon finely chopped fresh parsley

1 tablespoon butter

CHEESE CUSTARD

SERVES
4

250 ml/8 fl oz/1 cup milk

**100 g/4 oz/1 cup hard Irish
cheese, grated**

2 eggs, beaten

salt and freshly ground black pepper

Preheat the oven to 200°C/400°F/gas mark 6. Heat the milk and cheese in a flameproof, ovenproof pan, stirring until the cheese has dissolved. Stir in the beaten eggs and season with salt and pepper. Transfer to the oven and cook for 15 minutes until set, then serve hot.

FARMHOUSE CHEESE PARCELS

Preheat the oven to 190°C/375°F/gas mark 5. Place the filo sheets on the work surface and pile the cheeses on top, one on top of the other with the blue cheese in the centre. Moisten the edges of the pastry and seal into small parcels. Brush the parcels with the melted butter. Place seam-side down on a greased baking sheet and bake in the oven for 5–7 minutes until the cheese has melted and the pastry browned.

Make a salad by cutting the vegetables into julienne strips and dividing between individual plates. Liquidize all the dressing ingredients, then pour over the vegetable salad. Place a cheese parcel on each plate and serve at once.

4 x 15 cm (6 inch) square double sheets of filo pastry

4 x 75 g/3 oz slices of hard Irish cheese, cut into rectangles

4 x 75 g/3 oz slices of blue Irish cheese

4 x 75 g/3 oz slices of soft Irish cheese

3 tablespoons butter, melted

For the salad

2 parsnips

2 carrots

2 courgettes (zucchini)

For the dressing

175 ml/6 fl oz/¾ cup olive oil

4 tablespoons red wine vinegar

4 teaspoons caster (superfine) sugar

4 tablespoons chopped fresh mixed herbs

1 egg yolk

½ teaspoon salt

½ teaspoon freshly ground black pepper

BUTTERMILK PUDDING

SERVES
4

1 teaspoon powdered gelatine

2 tablespoons water

300 ml/½ pint/1¼ cups double
(heavy) cream

150 g/5 oz/⅔ cup caster
(superfine) sugar

1 vanilla pod (bean), halved

600 ml/1 pint/2½ cups buttermilk

Stir the gelatine into the water in a small bowl, then stand the bowl in a pan of hot water until the gelatine is transparent. Place half the cream, the sugar and vanilla pod in a saucepan and heat to just below boiling point. Remove from the heat and stir in the gelatine, blending well. Whisk the buttermilk into the hot cream. Remove the vanilla pod. Whisk the remaining cream until stiff, then fold into the hot mixture. Pour into a bowl, leave to cool, then chill well before serving.

IRISH EGGS BENEDICT

SERVES
4

Wrap the ham in baking foil and heat in a low oven. Poach the eggs and keep them warm. Toast the bread and keep it warm. To make the sauce, whisk the egg yolks and lemon juice until creamy, then very carefully and gradually pour in the melted butter, stirring constantly until it thickens. Place a warm ham slice on each of the warm bread slices and place a poached egg on top. Spoon the sauce over the eggs and garnish with the chives.

4 thick slices of cooked ham

4 eggs

4 thick slices of bread

2 teaspoons chopped fresh chives

For the sauce

2 egg yolks

2 teaspoons lemon juice

150 g/5 oz/⅔ cup butter, melted

Vegetables

One of the most common ingredients in cookery all over the world is the tomato, which originally comes from the maize fields of the Andes in South America. Originally considered a weed, this herbaceous plant was then grown for its fruit for thousands of years before it was discovered by the conquering Spanish and thence brought to Europe. The tomato (*Lycopersicum esculenta*) is a member of the Solanaceae family, which includes henbane, nightshade, chillies, peppers, aubergine (eggplant), tobacco and the potato. It grows well in most climates, and adapted itself even to the temperate climate of Ireland. Rich in vitamins A and C, iron and sugar, tomatoes are widely used in Irish sauces, relishes, pickles, chutneys and ketchup.

When it was first brought to Europe in the sixteenth century, the tomato was shunned by many because it was thought to be poisonous and the seeds were believed to cause appendicitis. Not only that, but Cromwell's Parliament believed it to be morally corrupting, and it became known as the *pomme d'amour*, or love apple.

Soft words butter no turnips, but neither will they harden the heart of a cabbage.

———

Old Irish saying

Like the potato and the tomato, maize – or sweetcorn – also arrived in Ireland from the Americas. Before the Great Famine of the nineteenth century, the average household of two adults and four children would eat 11 kg/24 lb of potatoes a week and most were almost entirely dependent on potatoes for their food. When the crops failed, the Irish looked to England to provide alternative food for the starving population. All they were offered was a maize meal made from the American corn cob. Many people were saved by making bread with the distinctive yellow flour and it remains a feature of local cooking.

Another native American product that has been introduced into Irish cookery is the sunflower. The oil, which is pressed from the flower's tiny, highly nutritious seeds, is widely used in cookery and sauces, and is light, with a faintly nutty flavour. Hulled sunflower seeds are also eaten raw and are high in protein and carbohydrates.

COLCANNON

———

Colcannon is similar to Champ (page 91), and the Irish make it with Comer potatoes from County Down. The dish is traditionally served at a family feast, when silver coins, or little charms, are hidden in the dish to be discovered by the children, in the same way that English cooks place silver coins in the Christmas pudding. There are variations of colcannon – some including onions instead of leeks, and parsnip or cabbage – and this recipe is a beautiful pale green colour because it is made with kale, a local crop that is cooked like cabbage. Diners dip their spoons into the melted butter before taking a spoonful of colcannon.

450 g/1 lb potatoes

450 g/1 lb curly kale, sliced

1 large leek, thinly sliced

150 ml/¼ pt/⅔ cup single (light) cream

¼ teaspoon salt

¼ teaspoon freshly ground black pepper

75 g/3 oz/⅓ cup butter, melted

Cook the potatoes in boiling water for about 15 minutes until tender, then drain and mash. Cook the kale in a little water for about 10 minutes until soft, then drain and chop finely. Simmer the leek in the cream for about 5 minutes until soft, then stir into the mashed potatoes with the kale and season with salt and pepper. Spoon the warm mixture into a deep dish and make a well in the centre. Pour the melted butter into the centre and serve.

IRISH CAULIFLOWER CHEESE

SERVES

4

1 large cauliflower

4 bay leaves

50 g/2 oz/¼ cup butter

1 large onion, sliced

2 tomatoes, peeled and sliced

25 g/1 oz/¼ cup plain
(all-purpose) flour

300 ml/½ pint/1¼ cups milk

1 teaspoon mustard

175 g/6 oz/1½ cups hard Irish
cheese, grated

¼ teaspoon salt

¼ teaspoon freshly ground
black pepper

4 eggs, separated

2 tablespoons fresh breadcrumbs

2 spring onions (scallions),
thinly sliced

Break the cauliflower head into florets, cutting out the stem. Steam the cauliflower over boiling water with the bay leaves for about 10 minutes until just tender, then drain and place in a flameproof dish. Melt half the butter and sauté the onion until soft. Add the tomatoes and cook for 3 minutes, then pour over the cauliflower. Melt the remaining butter and stir in the flour. Whisk in the milk, mustard, two-thirds of the cheese, and the salt and pepper. Pour over the cauliflower. Beat the egg whites until stiff, then place four large spoonfuls on top of the sauce. Make an indentation in each mound of egg white and fill them with the egg yolks. Scatter the breadcrumbs over the dish, then the rest of the cheese and the spring onions. Place under a hot grill for a few minutes until golden brown.

POTATO AND PARSNIP BAKE

SERVES
4

Preheat the oven to 180°C/350°F/gas mark 4. Arrange the vegetables in layers in a greased baking dish, dotting each layer with a little butter and seasoning with salt and pepper. Finish with a layer of potatoes. Pour over the milk or buttermilk, cover and bake in the oven for 1½ hours. Remove the cover and bake for a further 30 minutes to brown the potatoes.

450 g/1 lb potatoes, sliced
1 large onion, sliced
225 g/8 oz parsnips, sliced
50 g/2 oz/¼ cup butter
½ teaspoon salt
½ teaspoon freshly ground black pepper
300 ml/½ pint/1¼ cups milk or buttermilk

LEEK AND POTATO CASSEROLE

SERVES

4

450 g/1 lb potatoes, thinly sliced

450 g/1 lb leeks, cut into
4 cm (1½ inch) slices

40 g/1½ oz/3 tablespoons butter

25 g/1 oz/¼ cup wholemeal
(wholewheat) flour

300 ml/½ pint/1¼ cups milk

½ teaspoon mustard powder

¼ teaspoon freshly ground
black pepper

50 g/2 oz/½ cup hard Irish
cheese, grated

Preheat the oven to 200°C/400°F/gas mark 6. Cook the potatoes in boiling water for about 5 minutes until tender, then drain. Steam the leeks for about 10 minutes until just tender. Arrange the potatoes and leeks in a greased casserole dish. Melt the butter in a saucepan, stir in the flour and cook for 2 minutes, stirring, then whisk in the milk, mustard and pepper and cook over a low heat until thickened. Pour the sauce over the casserole and sprinkle with cheese. Bake in the oven for about 20 minutes until golden brown.

PARSNIP, CELERIAC AND POTATO MASH

SERVES

4

Celeriac is best known for the nutty flavour of its bulbous roots, and is one of many root crops – like parsnips and carrots – that are common ingredients in Irish cooking. The strong celery flavour of the celeriac and the sweet taste of the parsnip in this vegetable mash are both mellowed by the starchiness of the potatoes and the milk.

Place the vegetables in a saucepan and cover with cold water. Bring to the boil, then simmer for about 10 minutes until the potatoes are cooked. Drain well, then return them to the saucepan, add the milk, mustard and salt and pepper and mash together until smooth. Place over a low heat, add the butter and stir until it has melted into the vegetables.

350 g/12 oz potatoes, roughly chopped

225 g/8 oz celeriac, roughly chopped

225 g/ 8 oz parsnips, roughly chopped

175 ml/6 fl oz/¾ cup milk

½ teaspoon mustard

salt and freshly ground black pepper

75 g/3 oz/⅓ cup butter

CIDER ONION BAKE

SERVES

4

---

50 g/2 oz/¼ cup butter
4 onions, halved crossways
1 teaspoon dried thyme
½ teaspoon dried sage
½ teaspoon dried marjoram
¼ teaspoon salt
**¼ teaspoon freshly ground
black pepper**
4 tablespoons cider
**1 teaspoon finely chopped
fresh sage**

Wild marjoram (Origanum vulgare) *grows naturally in Ireland, but the most commonly used variety of this herb in Irish cooking is the garden variety* (Origanum onites)*. It goes well with almost everything except fish. Ironically, sweet marjoram* (Origanum marjorana) *used to be made into a tisaine to prevent sea-sickness, which was good for fishermen!*

Preheat the oven to 180°C/350°F/gas mark 4. Melt the butter in a flameproof, shallow casserole dish and sauté the onions flat-side down until browned. Remove from the heat, turn the onions flat-side up and sprinkle with thyme, sage, marjoram, salt and pepper. Pour the cider into the dish, cover and bake in the oven for 1 hour until tender, spooning the cooking liquid over the onions from time to time. Serve sprinkled with fresh sage.

PARSNIP BAKE

SERVES
4

Preheat the oven to 180°C/350°F/gas mark 4. Cook the parsnips in boiling water for about 15 minutes until half-cooked, then drain and place in an ovenproof dish. Add the stock and nutmeg and season with salt and pepper. Dot with the butter, then bake in the oven for 30 minutes until tender and golden brown.

450 g/1 lb parsnips, quartered
250 ml/8 fl oz/1 cup lamb
or chicken stock
a pinch of nutmeg
salt and freshly ground black pepper
25 g/1 oz/2 tablespoons butter

BRAISED IRISH CELERY

SERVES
4

100 g/4 oz streaky bacon, rinded

1 onion, sliced

1 carrot, sliced

10 celery sticks (stalks), without the leaves, cut into large chunks

300 ml/½ pint/1¼ cups chicken stock

1 bouquet garni

¼ teaspoon salt

¼ teaspoon freshly ground black pepper

Celery was introduced into Ireland in the seventeenth century from the Mediterranean, where it grew wild. Celery seeds are used in tomato juice and seafood dishes, pickles, chutneys, soups and stews, while the leaves and stalk are used as a vegetable, both cooked and uncooked.

Arrange the bacon in the bottom of a flameproof casserole dish and add the onion, carrot and celery. Pour in the stock, then add the bouquet garni, salt and pepper. Bring to the boil, cover and simmer gently for 1½ hours. Serve piping hot with Crubeens (page 136).

RED CABBAGE BAKE

SERVES

4

Sprinkle the cabbage with salt and leave to stand overnight until limp, then rinse and drain. Bring the wine, stock, vinegar and sugar to the boil in a saucepan. Add the peppercorns, thyme and garlic and return to the boil. Add the cabbage and boil for 2 minutes. Reduce the heat and simmer for 30 minutes. Serve hot as a vegetable, or cold with a salad.

1 small red cabbage, finely shredded

½ tablespoon salt

600 ml/1 pint/2½ cups red wine

300 ml/½ pint/1¼ cups
vegetable stock

150 ml/¼ pint/⅔ cup wine vinegar

75 g/3 oz/⅓ cup caster
(superfine) sugar

6 black peppercorns, crushed

1 teaspoon finely chopped
fresh thyme

2 garlic cloves, finely chopped

HORSERADISH TERRINE

SERVES

4

75 g/3 oz powdered gelatine

250 ml/8 fl oz/1 cup recently
boiled water

2 tablespoons grated horseradish

1 teaspoon grated lemon rind

½ teaspoon lemon juice

1 teaspoon salt

4 drops of green food colouring

3 tablespoons double (heavy) cream

Horseradish is the hot, peppery and pungent root of a vegetable which is often used in vinegars, chutneys and pickles but is best known as an accompaniment for beef. The roots were traditionally raised in November when they would be steeped in vinegar for use during the winter months. Since the juice can be irritating to the skin, you need to be careful when preparing it.

Dissolve the gelatine in recently boiled water, then stir in the horseradish, lemon rind, juice and salt. Let the mixture cool slightly, then whisk in the colouring. Whip the cream until stiff, then fold into the mixture. Pour into a mould and leave to set. Chill before serving.

TOMATO SAUCE

This sauce goes with just about everything. For a vegetarian version, omit the bacon and use a vegetable stock.

Melt half the butter in a saucepan and sauté the bacon for 2 minutes, then add the onion and carrot and sauté for 5 minutes. Add the tomatoes, cover and cook for 5 minutes. Stir in the stock and bring to the boil. Mix the flour and water to a paste, then stir it into the pan with the sugar, lemon juice, salt and pepper. Cover and simmer for 30 minutes. Leave to cool, then rub through a sieve. Reheat the sauce and stir in the remaining butter.

50 g/2 oz/¼ cup butter

1 bacon rasher (slice), rinded and chopped

1 onion, finely chopped

1 carrot, thinly sliced

450 g/1 lb ripe tomatoes, peeled and quartered

300 ml/½ pint/1¼ cups chicken stock

1 tablespoon plain (all-purpose) flour

3 tablespoons water

1 teaspoon caster (superfine) sugar

½ teaspoon lemon juice

¼ teaspoon salt

¼ teaspoon freshly ground black pepper

Meat

Pork and ham figure substantially in Irish cookery, with Irish bacon forming an integral part of the Ulster fry, the day's first meal. In olden times, most homesteads had at least one pig, which would often live in the cottage itself. Anthony Trollope, the celebrated author who spent several years in Ireland, set his 1844 novel *The Kellys and O'Kellys* in the village of Dunmore in Connacht. He vividly describes the Irish country kitchen and its occupants: two pigs, a cockerel, three or four chickens, a dog and a heap of potatoes. Pigs are so important a part of the Irish way of life that the first annual pig race, held in Naas in County Kildare, attracted a crowd of 7,000 spectators and speculators. Bookies donated their profits to charity, and the fastest trotters on the course belonged to a pig aptly named Porky's Revenge. Crubeens, a traditional Irish dish, is made from pigs' trotters, but hopefully not from a race competitor!

Until quite recently, the traditional Irish peasant's cabin, or cottage, was a one-roomed, turf-thatched, stone-built structure. On the bleak west coast, these were

May the grass grow green before your door.

———

Early Irish curse

sometimes set into the ground to offer more protection from the prevailing weather. Inside, the floor was of baked earth and the focal point was the turf fire. An iron pot, used for boiling potatoes, would stand on an iron griddle, used for cooking. A bed stood to the right of the fire, with four roof-high posts at each corner, to which straw mats were fitted for warmth and modesty. Other furniture consisted of four posts in the floor with wicker sides, serving as a potato bin, and deal shelves beside the bed, which were used as a dresser. There would be a few crude wooden stools and a chair made of straw. To one side of the door were pegs on which to hang cloaks, the main item of outdoor clothing, and above the door was a wicker-work hen-coop. This family home would usually be shared by a cow or one or more pigs, although one traveller in Ireland in 1837 remarked that he sometimes saw cabins so poor that there was not even one pig in them.

Turf fires are still common in the cottages out in the wilds of Ireland, and turf and peat cutters still operate, especially in the west of the country. Cutting turf for fuel is a time-consuming job. The turf is cut with a spade known as a *slane*, then spread out on a turf field. The process then involves footing, or stacking six turfs in a pyramid shape; rickling, or stacking the turfs on their sides; clamping, or stacking heaps of turfs near the access path; and finally, drawing them home to the cottage. The field work, apart from the cutting, was usually done by women and children, and the drawing home was by the traditional Irish horse-drawn cart or *carr*.

During the Iron Age, farmers fearing cattle rustlers on the shores of Lough Gara in Roscommon built artificial islands, or *crannogs*, in the lake. Around 300 of these islets exist, and dugout canoes were used to ferry the cattle over to the islets. *Crannogs* were in use up until the 1600s.

In colloquial Gaelic, joints of meat were sometimes known as *sproals*, and small joints went by the name of *spoileens*. *Spoileens* was also the term used for travelling commercial kitchens. These were in the form of tents, in which two fires heated large pots of *spoileen*, a type of boiled mutton stew sold with bread. These *spoileen* tents would be found in fairgrounds and at any public celebrations, and were very popular across Ireland during the mid-nineteenth century. They were also probably a feature of Cork's famous Old English Market, which dates back to the late eighteenth century.

Mutton is the meat of a sheep over 18 months old; animals younger than that yield lamb. Some of the best lamb comes from the mountains and valleys where heather mingles with wild herbs, imparting a subtle hint of the moors and peat bogs and their wild flowers. Most mutton brought for the home table is between three and four years old. Mutton is very popular in Irish recipes and the local mutton is firm textured and close grained. Salt-meadow mutton is favoured, the animals being raised on pastures rich in wild herbs, clover and shamrock. In the eighteenth century, some lamb recipes were most ambitious and often recommended seafood as an accompaniment. One popular stuffing for mutton and lamb consisted of oysters, crab meat and anchovies. Some early local recipes also suggested that carragheen, the Irish seaweed, went well with mutton.

Veal comes from two- to three-month-old calves which have been especially milk-fed. It is a tender, pink, firm flesh, and a noted delicacy. There are eight different cuts of veal, but the thin, tender escalopes, from the leg of the calf, are the most popular and the tastiest part of the animal. Probably the finest veal in Ireland comes from County Kerry, which is almost the only place you will find the native Kerry cattle. There is a proverb in both County Kerry and County Donegal which says: 'Kerry cows know Sunday.' This evolved from the tradition of taking blood from the cows to boil into a mixture with sorrel, making a wholesome broth for Sunday lunch when the peasant folk had no other food.

The Irish are avid smokers of food – apart from the classic image of Irish pub-goers with clay pipes in their mouths! In many country cottages a smoked ham or two hangs from the beams. Smoke-houses exist all over Ireland. The Irish seem to smoke anything that runs, swims or flies, from beef and pork to pheasant and chicken, and from salmon, haddock and eel to trout, cod and herring. There are more than a dozen smoke-houses in Ireland which smoke ham in the traditional way.

Particularly popular in County Cork, drisheen is the name for a rich, dark blood sausage, or black pudding. A white variety is unique to County Cork, where it is often served with tripe and can be made with lambs' blood. Commercially, drisheen is made by combining pigs' blood with finely minced pork fat trimmings, onions and herbs. Oatmeal or breadcrumbs are often added, and usually some cream and herbs such as mace or tansy. This mixture is then poured through a funnel into a length of pig's gut to form a long coil. The sausage is brushed with blood, which turns black when cooked, and boiled or poached until the blood sets. When drisheen is made at home, a shallow, wide pan is used in which to steam-bake the sausage in an oven.

SERVES

4

CRUBEENS

4 pigs' trotters

1 onion, halved

1 carrot, quartered

6 peppercorns, crushed

1 bay leaf

½ tablespoon chopped fresh parsley

1 teaspoon chopped fresh thyme

¼ teaspoon salt

Place all the ingredients in a large pan and cover with cold water. Bring to the boil, then cover and simmer for 3 hours. Serve hot as a stew with Guinness and brown soda bread, or cold with salad.

TRADITIONAL ULSTER FRY

This scrambled egg and bacon dish is a crucial element in the classic Ulster fry, in which it is served with grilled bacon, black pudding, farmhouse sausages, tomatoes, mushrooms and lambs' kidneys. Fried eggs make a good alternative.

Fry the bacon in a dry pan until crisp. Whisk the eggs in a bowl with the cream and pepper. Mix with the bacon and scramble over a gentle heat. Before it sets, add the cheese and chives and stir together.

4 streaky bacon rashers (slices), rinded and chopped

6 eggs

2 tablespoons single (light) cream

½ teaspoon black pepper

25 g/1 oz/¼ cup hard Irish cheese, grated

1 tablespoon chopped fresh chives

ROAST HERB LAMB

SERVES

4–6

1.5 kg/3 lb leg of lamb, trimmed
1 onion, chopped
150 ml/¼ pint/⅔ cup water
3 tablespoons white wine
salt and freshly ground black pepper

For the topping
2 large garlic cloves
4 teaspoons grated root ginger
grated rind of 1 lemon
2 tablespoons chopped
fresh parsley
2 tablespoons chopped fresh mint
1 tablespoon chopped
fresh rosemary
2 tablespoons olive oil

Preheat the oven to 180°C/350°F/gas mark 4. Briefly blend the garlic, ginger, lemon rind, parsley, mint and rosemary to a fine mixture. Stir in the olive oil and blend to a paste. Place the joint in a roasting tin with the onion and water and cook in the oven for 45 minutes. Remove from the oven and spread the herb mixture over the joint. Return to the oven and cook for a further 30 minutes, topping up with water if necessary, until the lamb is cooked. Remove the meat from the pan and keep it warm. Discard the onion. Stir the wine into the pan juices, bring to the boil and simmer for a few minutes until reduced, stirring in all the cooking juices. Season with salt and pepper. Slice the lamb and serve with the gravy and Mint Sauce (page 139).

MINT SAUCE

———

Mint sauce is traditionally served with roast lamb or mutton dishes and is usually made with spearmint (Mentha spicata), *although there are a number of other varieties of mint, including peppermint and applemint. Mint sauces can be made in any number of ways, but the basic recipe combines the flavour of mint with vinegar and sugar, although some prefer it tart, without the sugar.*

Pound the mint with the sugar in a mortar, then set aside for 30 minutes. Add the boiling water and stir until the sugar has dissolved, then stir in the vinegar.

2 tablespoons finely chopped fresh mint

2 teaspoons caster (superfine) sugar

1 tablespoon boiling water

4 tablespoons malt vinegar

MOUNTAIN MUTTON POT ROAST

SERVES

4–6

1.5 kg/3 lb leg of mutton, boned

2 tablespoons corn oil

1 onion, sliced

2 celery sticks (stalks), sliced

4 carrots, halved

450 g/1 lb new potatoes

6 tablespoons mutton stock

¼ teaspoon salt

¼ teaspoon freshly ground black pepper

For the stuffing

225 g/8 oz sausage meat

1 onion, chopped

1 tablespoon finely chopped fresh parsley

2 teaspoons dried oregano

1 garlic clove, crushed

It is recorded that in 1780 a Reverend James Kenny was building a herb garden in Kilnanahee, where he grew balm, sage, thyme, pennyroyal, rosemary, camomile and horehound, amongst other herbs. This testifies to the great interest in both culinary and medicinal herbs in Ireland, and the fact that they form an important part of the culinary heritage.

Preheat the oven to 160°C/325°F/gas mark 3. Mix together all the stuffing ingredients and use to stuff the mutton leg. Heat the oil in a flameproof casserole and brown the leg all over. Add the vegetables and stock and season with salt and pepper. Cover the casserole and cook in the oven for 2 hours until the mutton is tender. Slice the meat and serve with the vegetables.

STOUT BRAISED BEEF

———

Preheat the oven to 190°C/375°F/gas mark 5. Heat the oil and sauté the onions until soft, then transfer to a casserole dish using a slotted spoon and add the carrots. Season the flour with salt and pepper and roll the beef in it. Brown the meat in the oil, then transfer to the casserole. Add the rest of the flour to the oil left in the pan and cook for 2 minutes, then stir in the stout and basil. Bring to the boil, then add the stock and honey. Stir well, then pour over the meat, cover the dish and cook in the oven for about 1½ hours until the meat is tender and the gravy has thickened. Serve with Horseradish Cream Sauce (page 142).

3 tablespoons vegetable oil

3 onions, chopped

4 carrots, halved and sliced lengthways

3 tablespoons plain (all-purpose) flour

salt and freshly ground black pepper

700 g/1½ lb beef steak, cut into 10 pieces

150 ml/¼ pint/⅔ cup Irish stout

½ teaspoon finely chopped fresh basil

150 ml/¼ pint/⅔ cup beef stock

1 teaspoon clear honey

SERVES

4

HORSERADISH CREAM SAUCE

3 tablespoons freshly grated
horseradish

1 teaspoon mustard

1 teaspoon sugar

1 teaspoon lemon juice

½ teaspoon salt

¼ teaspoon freshly ground
black pepper

2 teaspoons vinegar

300 ml/½ pint/1¼ cups double
(heavy) cream

Mix together all the ingredients except the cream. Whip the cream until stiff, then fold it into the sauce and serve.

STEAK AND KIDNEY PUDDING

———

Reserve a quarter of the pastry, then roll out the remainder on a lightly floured board and use to line a greased pudding bowl. Season the flour with salt and pepper, then coat the meat and kidneys in the flour, mix with the onion and put them into the basin. Pour in the stout. Roll out the reserved pastry to make a lid, dampen the edges with water and seal the pastry lid to the base. Cover with greaseproof paper and secure with string. Place the pudding in a large saucepan and fill with hot water to come half way up the sides of the basin. Cover and steam for 4 hours, topping up with boiling water as necessary, then serve piping hot.

225 g/8 oz suet pastry

2 tablespoons plain (all-purpose) flour

salt and freshly ground black pepper

350 g/12 oz stewing steak, cubed

100 g/4 oz kidney, trimmed and quartered

1 onion, finely chopped

3 tablespoons Irish stout

KERRY KIDNEYS

50 g/2 oz/¼ cup butter

2 onions, sliced

225 g/8 oz small sausages, halved

8 lambs' kidneys, cored, cleaned
and halved

1 tablespoon plain
(all-purpose) flour

300 ml/½ pint/1¼ cups stock

300 ml/½ pint/1¼ cups Irish stout

1 tablespoon tomato purée (paste)

¼ teaspoon salt

¼ teaspoon freshly ground
black pepper

225 g/8 oz button mushrooms, sliced

Preheat the oven to 160°C/325°F/gas mark 3. Melt the butter and sauté the onions until golden brown, then add the sausages and cook for 1 minute. Add the kidneys and sauté until browned, then turn all the ingredients into a casserole dish. Stir the flour into the butter remaining in the pan and cook over a low heat until brown, then add the stock, stout and tomato purée. Stir well and season with salt and pepper. Bring to the boil, then pour into the casserole. Cover and cook in the oven for 1½ hours. Add the mushrooms, then return to the oven for 15 minutes until the meat is tender and the gravy is thick.

BACON AND
POTATO SUPPER

Place the sausages, bacon and stock in a saucepan, bring to the boil, then simmer for 5 minutes. Add all the remaining ingredients except the chives, season with salt and pepper and return to the boil. Cover and simmer gently for 1 hour until the meat is cooked and the stew has thickened. Sprinkle the chives over the top and serve immediately.

450 g/1 lb pork sausages

8 thick back bacon rashers (slices), rinded

1.2 litres/2 pints/5 cups vegetable stock

8 potatoes, sliced

4 onions, sliced

3 tablespoons chopped fresh parsley

¼ teaspoon salt

¼ teaspoon freshly ground black pepper

2 teaspoons finely chopped chives

TRADITIONAL BACON AND CABBAGE SUPPER

1 large Savoy cabbage, separated into leaves

10 bacon rashers (slices), rinded

5 allspice berries

salt and freshly ground black pepper

300 ml/½ pint/1¼ cups ham stock

Cook the cabbage in boiling salted water for 15 minutes. Drain, soak in cold water for 1 minute, then drain again and slice. Line an ovenproof dish with 5 bacon rashers, cover with the cabbage and sprinkle with allspice, salt and pepper. Lay the rest of the bacon on top and pour over the stock. Bring to the boil, cover and simmer for 1 hour until the stock has been absorbed. Serve hot.

HAM, PEA
AND POTATO SUPPER

Melt half the butter in a large saucepan and gently sauté the onion for 3 minutes. Add the stock, ham and peas. Bring up to a simmer and add the potatoes. Mix together the milk, mustard and cornflour into a paste, then stir it into the stew with the thyme and parsley. Simmer gently, without boiling, for 8 minutes. Season with the pepper, and stir in the rest of the butter. When the butter has melted, serve hot with soda bread.

50 g/2 oz/¼ cup butter

1 onion, chopped

600 ml/1 pint/2½ cups ham stock

175 g/6 oz smoked ham, diced

100 g/4 oz peas

225 g/8 oz boiled potatoes, diced

4 tablespoons milk

½ teaspoon mustard

½ tablespoon cornflour (cornstarch)

¼ teaspoon thyme

**½ tablespoon finely chopped
fresh parsley**

**¼ teaspoon freshly ground
black pepper**

GAMMON
WITH WHISKEY SAUCE

SERVES

4

4 gammon steaks, trimmed of fat

2 tablespoons unsalted
(sweet) butter

½ tablespoon salted butter, softened

½ onion, finely chopped or grated

2 tablespoons plain
(all-purpose) flour

175 ml/6 fl oz/¾ cup vegetable stock

1 teaspoon soft brown sugar

2 teaspoons Irish whiskey

salt and freshly ground black pepper

Brush half the unsalted butter over one side of the steaks, then grill the steaks on the buttered side for 7 minutes. Turn the steaks, brush with the remaining butter and grill the other side. Meanwhile, heat the salted butter and sauté the onion until golden. Remove from the heat and stir in the flour, then blend in the stock. Return to the heat and add the sugar. Bring to the boil, stirring, then simmer for 2 minutes. Add the whiskey, salt and pepper and simmer until hot and well blended. Serve the gammon steaks with the sauce poured over them.

LIMERICK HAM

In County Limerick, ham was traditionally smoked over a fire containing juniper berries and leaves, giving it a particular flavour recognized universally since the 1700s. Blue-black juniper berries are also used to flavour game and meat dishes, especially stews, and are added to marinades for pork and lamb dishes. They are also one of the distinctive flavours of gin and are infused in water to make a medicinal tea. They are often crushed before use to release the flavours. Juniper's Latin name is Juniperus communis *and it is part of the cypress family.*

Preheat the oven to 200°C/400°F/gas mark 6. Deeply score the ham all over with a knife. Rub the juniper berries into the cuts, pushing them in. Mix together the gin, sugar and mustard. Cover the ham all over with the mixture. Place in an ovenproof dish and cover with baking foil. Bake in the oven for about 20 minutes until heated through. Remove the foil and bake for a further 20 minutes or so until the skin is crisp, basting regularly with the liquid produced.

1 ham on the bone, cured and cooked

25 g/1 oz/¼ cup juniper berries

250 ml/8 fl oz/1 cup gin

250 ml/8 fl oz/1 cup soft brown sugar

175 g/6 oz/⅔ cup coarse-grain mustard

SERVES

4

DRISHEEN

1.2 litres/2 pints/5 cups
sheep's blood (obtainable from
some local butchers)

225 g/8 oz/2 cups oatmeal

2 teaspoons salt

600 ml/1 pint/2½ cups full
cream milk

1 tablespoon single (light) cream

¼ teaspoon chopped fresh tansy

¼ teaspoon freshly ground
black pepper

This traditional Irish black pudding is flavoured with tansy. Tansy (Tanacetum vulgare) is a perennial European herb which is often used in cooking as a substitute for nutmeg and cinnamon in desserts, and in soups and stews. Tansy tea is made from an infusion of the leaves, which is one of the most popular traditional herbal teas despite its slightly bitter taste.

Strain the blood into a bowl, and mix in all the remaining ingredients. Leave to stand for about an hour. Pour into a greased dish and cover with baking foil. Place in a large baking dish and pour enough boiling water around the dish to come half way up the sides. Bake in the oven at 160°C/325°F/gas mark 3 for about 30 minutes until set. Serve sliced.

GOOSEBERRY DRISHEEN SAUSAGES

Blend the drisheen or black pudding, spring onions, peppers, potatoes, mustard, vinegar, salt and pepper in a food processor. Shape the mixture into little sausage shapes about 7.5 cm (3 inches) long. Roll them in the flour, then the eggs and then in the breadcrumbs. Heat the oil and sauté the sausages until golden brown. Drain and keep warm.

To make the compote, dissolve the sugar in the water, bring to the boil and simmer for a few minutes to make a syrup. Add the gooseberries and cook for 10 minutes until soft. Strain off any excess juice and pour over the black pudding sausages to serve.

225 g/8 oz drisheen or other black pudding, peeled and roughly chopped

6 spring onions (scallions), finely chopped

2 red (bell) peppers, seeded and diced

175 g/6 oz mashed potatoes

2 tablespoons mustard

2 tablespoons malt vinegar

¼ teaspoon salt

¼ teaspoon freshly ground black pepper

225 g/8 oz/2 cups plain (all-purpose) flour

4 eggs, lightly beaten

225 g/8 oz/4 cups fresh white breadcrumbs

3 tablespoons vegetable oil

For the compote

350 g/12 oz/1½ cups caster (superfine) sugar

600 ml/1 pint/2½ cups water

225 g/8 oz gooseberries

151

SERVES

4

CABBAGE AND CORNED BEEF

—————

900 g/2 lb corned beef brisket

1 onion

6 cloves

1 tablespoon chopped fresh parsley

½ teaspoon dried thyme

450 g/1 lb cabbage, coarsely shredded

4 potatoes, quartered

3 carrots, halved

For the sauce

150 ml/¼ pint/⅔ cup double (heavy) cream

1 tablespoon mayonnaise

3 tablespoons grated horseradish

Place the meat in a saucepan, cover with water and bring to the boil. Press the cloves into the onion and add to the pan with the parsley and thyme and simmer for 1 hour. Skim the surface. Add the cabbage, potatoes and carrots. Simmer for about 25 minutes until the vegetables are cooked. Take off the heat, lift the meat out of the pan and cut it into chunks. Strain the vegetables and serve with the meat.

To make the sauce, whip the cream until stiff, then fold in the mayonnaise and horseradish. Serve with the meat and vegetables.

HONEY-GLAZED HAM

———

Soak the ham in water overnight, then drain. Stud the onion with the cloves, place in a large saucepan with the ham and cover with water. Add the peppercorns and half the honey and bring to the boil. Skim off the scum, then simmer for about 1 hour and 20 minutes. Remove the ham from the pan and peel off the skin. Replace in the stock and allow to cool, then drain. Heat the sugar, vinegar and the remaining honey, stirring until mixed. Pour the mixture over the drained ham and leave to cool. Then serve thinly sliced.

1 x 1.5 kg/3 lb piece of
smoked ham
1 large onion
8 cloves
6 peppercorns, crushed
3 tablespoons clear honey
2 tablespoons soft brown sugar
2 tablespoons vinegar

SERVES

4–6

SPICY ROAST PORK

1.5 kg/3 lb pork belly

2 tablespoons oil

For the stuffing

75 g/3 oz/⅓ cup butter

1 onion, finely chopped

3 garlic cloves, crushed

225 g/8 oz/4 cups fine fresh
breadcrumbs

1 teaspoon finely chopped mixed
fresh herbs

1 egg, beaten

¼ teaspoon salt

¼ teaspoon freshly ground
black pepper

For the paste

2 tablespoons melted butter

2 tablespoons chutney

2 garlic cloves, crushed

1 tablespoon lemon juice

2 tablespoons mustard

This stuffed and rolled pork joint makes a delicious meal, served with seasonal vegetables and accompanied by a home-made Apple Sauce (page 155).

Preheat the oven to 180°/350°F/gas mark 4. To make the stuffing, heat the butter and sauté the onion and garlic until soft. Remove from the heat, stir in the breadcrumbs and herbs and leave to cool. Mix in the egg to bind the stuffing and season with salt and pepper. Mix together the paste ingredients. Prick the meat all over with a fork and rub half the paste all over the inside of the meat. Spread the stuffing over the meat, then roll it up with the stuffing inside and tie with string. Heat the oil in a roasting tin and brown the meat all over, then turn the meat seam-side up, transfer the pan to the oven and cook for 1½ hours. Remove the meat from the oven, brush the outside with the rest of the paste and turn seam-side down. Return to the oven and cook for a further 1½ hours. Serve sliced.

CLASSIC APPLE SAUCE

———

The sharp flavour of apple sauce perfectly complements the richness of roast pork and this recipe is perfect to serve with Spicy Roast Pork (page 154).

Place the apples in a saucepan and rinse with water, then drain, leaving just the water clinging to the fruit. Add the cloves and lemon rind and cook gently for about 10 minutes until soft. Stir in the sugar and cook until dissolved. Rub the sauce through a sieve to make a purée. Stir in the butter and reheat gently to serve, or leave to cool.

450 g/1 lb cooking (tart) apples, peeled, cored and sliced

4 cloves

grated rind of ¼ lemon

2 tablespoons caster (superfine) sugar

1 tablespoon butter

Poultry and Game

In 1698, John Dunton, an English traveller in Ireland, recounted his experiences of staying with the Offlaghertie family. He was invited to walk a short distance to view their deer and was surprised to hear of a deer park in the wild place in which they were staying. However, after trekking through bogs and over mountains, the group came to Glinglass Vale, or the Green Valley, where they came across 'some hundreds of stately red deer, the stags bigger than a large English yearling calfe, with suitable antlers much bigger than I ever saw before.' Dunton recounts it as the most pleasing scene he met with in the kingdom and after the group had retired for a vast beef and mutton dinner, 'myn host ordered his dogs to be gotten ready to hunt the stagg.'

Yet may this cup of whey,
O Lord, serve as my
ale-feast
Fathoming its bitterness,
I'll learn that you know
best.

———

Attributed to the Hag of Beare

HONEY-TRUSSED CHICKEN

1 x 1.5 kg/3 lb chicken
1 teaspoon coarse sea salt
1 lemon, halved
4 bay leaves, crushed
2 sprigs of fresh rosemary
3 tablespoons olive oil
2 tablespoons clear honey
¼ teaspoon salt
¼ teaspoon freshly ground
black pepper
1 tablespoon chopped fresh parsley
½ tablespoon chopped fresh basil
½ tablespoon chopped
fresh marjoram

Preheat the oven to 200°C/400°F/gas mark 6. Rub the cavity of the chicken with the sea salt. Place half of the lemon inside the cavity, add the bay leaves and rosemary sprigs, then the second piece of lemon. Carefully tear back the skin from the top of the chicken breast. Mix together the olive oil and honey and season with salt and pepper. Rub half the mixture over the exposed breast. Mix together the parsley, basil and marjoram and sprinkle half the mixture over the top, then replace the skin over the breast. Slash the thighs three times on each side and rub the remaining herb mixture into the cuts. Rub the remaining honey and oil mixture over the chicken skin. Place the chicken, breast-side up in a baking dish. Cook in the oven for 10 minutes, then turn the chicken breast-side down and cook for 10 more minutes. Turn the chicken breast-side up and cook for about 1 hour until the juices run clear when pierced in the thickest part with a skewer.

WILD DUCK
WITH BABY TURNIPS

Arrange the bacon, celery, carrots, onions and bay leaf in a flameproof casserole dish and place the duck on top. Cook over a low heat for 10 minutes. Pour over the cider, bring to the boil and simmer until the cider has reduced by half. Pour over the stock, bring to the boil, cover and simmer very gently for 1 hour until the duck is tender. Meanwhile, cook the turnips in boiling salted water for 10 minutes. Remove the duck from the casserole and set aside. Skim off any fat from the surface of the dish, then rub the vegetables and liquid through a sieve to make a sauce and return it to the dish. Place the duck back in the dish and add the turnips. Heat through until the duck is very hot, then serve immediately.

4 bacon rashers (slices), rinded
1 celery stick (stalk), chopped
3 carrots, sliced
2 onions, sliced into rings
1 bay leaf
1 x 1.75 kg/4 lb oven-ready wild duck
300 ml/½ pint/1¼ cups dry cider
300 ml/½ pint/1¼ cups brown stock
24 whole baby turnips
¼ teaspoon salt

GAELIC ROAST GOOSE

SERVES

8

1 x 3.5 kg/8 lb oven-ready goose

25 g/1 oz/2 tablespoons butter

1 teaspoon salt

½ teaspoon freshly ground
black pepper

¼ teaspoon ground ginger

600 ml/1 pint/2½ cups stock

150 ml/¼ pint/⅔ cup port

1 lemon, quartered

For the stuffing

2 onions, finely chopped

450 g/1 lb potatoes, boiled
and mashed

225 g/8 oz sausage meat

120 ml/4 fl oz/½ cup double
(heavy) cream

2 teaspoons dried sage

½ teaspoon salt

½ teaspoon freshly ground
black pepper

*The best goose to cook is one that is no more than a year old.
As a lot of fat is exuded from a roasting goose, the amount of
meat is comparatively small, and you will need quite a large
bird to serve four people. The fat should regularly be removed
from the roasting tin whilst cooking.*

Preheat the oven to 180°C/350°F/gas mark 4. Mix together
the stuffing ingredients and fill the goose. Truss the bird
tightly, sewing each end. Mix the butter with the salt,
pepper and ginger and spread this mixture over the breast.
Place in a roasting tin and pour over the stock. Cook in the
oven for 2 hours, pouring off excess fat from time to time.
Stir the port into the cooking juices and return to the oven
for a further 30 minutes until the goose is tender and the
skin is crisp.

POT ROAST PHEASANT

Savory is used here in a bouquet garni with other herbs to bring out the gamey flavour of pheasant. Both originally natives of southern Europe, the two varieties of savory, Satureia hortensis *and* Satureia montana, *are both features of Irish herb gardens. As well as game dishes, the herb can be found in many recipes for pulses, meat and poultry, while in the past the oil was used as a remedy for insect bites and stings.*

Preheat the oven to 150°C/300°F/gas mark 2. Heat the oil and butter in a frying pan and brown the pheasant on all sides. Transfer the pheasant to a casserole dish and add the apple quarters. Add the onion to the pan and sauté until soft. Stir in the flour and cook for 1 minute, then add the stock, wine, sugar and orange juice and bring to the boil, stirring until smooth. Season with salt and pepper and pour over the pheasant. Tie the herbs into a bundle and add to the dish. Cover the casserole and cook in the oven for 1 hour until the juices run clear when you pierce the thickest part of the meat with a skewer. Discard the herbs before serving.

2 tablespoons vegetable oil

1 tablespoon butter

1 large oven-ready pheasant

2 eating (dessert) apples, peeled, cored and quartered

1 onion, chopped

4 teaspoons plain (all-purpose) flour

150 ml/¼ pint/⅔ cup stock

150 ml/¼ pint/⅔ cup red wine

1 tablespoon soft brown sugar

juice of 1 orange

¼ teaspoon salt

¼ teaspoon freshly ground black pepper

1 bay leaf

1 sprig of fresh thyme

1 sprig of fresh savory

2 sprigs of fresh parsley

SERVES

4

225 g/8 oz shallots

100 g/4 oz streaky bacon,
rinded and diced

2 oven-ready partridges

225 g/8 oz button mushrooms,
stalks removed

600 ml/1 pint/2½ cups stock

¼ tablespoon finely chopped
fresh lovage

225 g/8 oz/1 cup butter

1 tablespoon plain
(all-purpose) flour

juice of ½ lemon

salt and freshly ground black pepper

PEASANT'S PARTRIDGE POT

Lovage (Levisticum officinale) *probably arrived in Ireland with the Romans, as it was one of their favourite herbs. It has a warm, aromatic flavour, and the stems, seeds and leaves of the plant are all used in soups, stews, casseroles and salads. It used to be the main flavouring in a cordial which was once popular as a digestive, and lovage tea, either savoury or sweet, is still served in Ireland.*

Preheat the oven to 150°C/300°F/gas mark 2. Finely chop and reserve two of the shallots. Cook half the bacon in a flameproof casserole dish until the fat runs, then add the partridges and cook until browned all over. Add the whole shallots and the mushroom caps. Pour in half the stock, add the lovage, cover and transfer to the oven for 2 hours.

Meanwhile, heat the butter and sauté the rest of the bacon and the chopped shallots until browned. Add the mushroom stalks, stir in the flour and cook for 1 minute, stirring. Whisk in the remaining stock, bring to the boil and simmer until thick. Stir in the lemon juice and season with salt and pepper. Lift the partridge and vegetables from the casserole and arrange on a serving dish. Discard any fat and keep warm. Stir a little of the cooking juices from the partridge into the sauce until it is the consistency you prefer. Pour over the partridges to serve.

HOMESTEAD RABBIT PIE

———

Originally from southern Europe, the blueish-green sage
(Salvia officinalis) *grows well in Ireland and is widely
used in cookery. As it has a very pungent flavour, it should
always be used sparingly whether fresh or dried. The stout
in this dish gives it a typically Irish bite, and sage is the
ideal complement to wild Irish rabbit.*

Preheat the oven to 200°C/400°F/gas mark 6. Melt half
the butter and sauté the rabbit portions until browned on
all sides, then remove from the pan. Add the onion, bacon
and mushrooms to the pan and fry until softened, then
return the rabbit to the pan and pour over the stout. Bring
to the boil, cover and simmer for about 15 minutes. Blend
the stock with the cornflour, salt and pepper, stir into the
pan and simmer, stirring until thickened. Continue to
cook for a further 15 minutes until the rabbit is tender.
Spoon into a greased ovenproof dish. Roll out the pastry
on a lightly floured board and press over the dish, sealing
the edges and decorating with the pastry trimmings. Make
a hole in the centre of the pastry for steam to escape and
brush the top with the milk. Bake in the oven for about
20 minutes until the pastry is golden brown.

50 g/2 oz/¼ cup butter

4 rabbit portions

1 onion, chopped

**50 g/2 oz bacon, rinded and
chopped**

175 g/6 oz mushrooms, sliced

150 ml/¼ pint/⅔ cup Irish stout

150 ml/¼ pint/⅔ cup chicken stock

**2 tablespoons cornflour
(cornstarch)**

¼ teaspoon salt

**¼ teaspoon freshly ground
black pepper**

175 g/6 oz puff pastry

1 tablespoon milk

POACHER'S JUGGED WILD HARE

SERVES

4

1 hare, jointed

900 ml/1½ pints/3¾ cups Irish stout

6 peppercorns, crushed

1 bay leaf

2 tablespoons corn oil

50 g/2 oz/¼ cup butter

3 streaky bacon rashers (slices), rinded

450 g/1 lb small onions, roughly chopped

1 garlic clove crushed with 1 teaspoon salt

½ tablespoon plain (all-purpose) flour

½ teaspoon dried basil

½ teaspoon dried oregano

3 tablespoons chicken stock

25 g/1 oz/2 tablespoons margarine

225 g/8 oz button mushrooms

Sweet basil (Ocimum basilicum) *and bush basil* (Ocimum minimum) *are the varieties most commonly used in Irish cooking. Traditionally used in tomato, meat, egg or cheese dishes, basil also gives a wonderful depth to this hare recipe. Unlike rabbit, hare is a dark, rich meat more akin to other game.*

Place the hare in a dish, pour over the stout and add the peppercorns, bay leaf and oil. Cover and leave to stand in a cool place overnight. Remove from the marinade and pat dry on kitchen paper. Heat the butter in a large saucepan and sauté the bacon for 3 minutes. Add the hare and sauté until browned, then remove from the pan. Add half the onions and the crushed garlic and sauté until softened, then return the hare to the pan. Sprinkle with the flour, basil and oregano and cook for 1 minute. Strain in the marinade, add the stock and bring to the boil. Cover and simmer for 3 hours until the hare is very tender, adding a little more stout or stock if necessary during cooking. Heat the margarine and lightly sauté the remaining onions and the mushrooms until just golden. Remove the hare from the pan and keep warm. Add the fried onions and mushrooms to the sauce and heat, uncovered, for a few minutes until reduced and thickened, then pour over the hare to serve.

WHISKEY-GRILLED WILD BOAR STEAKS

SERVES

4

Wild boar used to be common in Ireland and the traditional Christmas dish of the nobility was stuffed wild boar's head served with bay and rosemary sprigs. Rosemary (Rosmarinus officinalis) *is a commonly used herb with game, lamb and pork dishes, as it has a strong flavour. The saying 'rosemary for remembrance' has come about because it is supposed to improve the memory, as well as having other medicinal qualities. It is a good complement to the rich, gamey flavour of wild boar, which was a favourite with the legendary Irish warrior kings. Boar have not been seen in Britain or Ireland for many centuries, but cuts can now be obtained from specialist shops. The recipe will work with pork, although the flavour will be different.*

6 juniper berries, crushed

2 tablespoons vegetable oil

1 tablespoon clear honey

1 tablespoon Irish whiskey

½ teaspoon paprika

¼ teaspoon salt

¼ teaspoon freshly ground black pepper

4 x 225 g/8 oz wild boar steaks

4 sprigs of fresh rosemary

Mix together the juniper berries, oil, honey, whiskey, paprika, salt and pepper. Brush the steaks on both sides with the mixture. Place one steak on a large piece of baking foil and pile the rest of the steaks on top of each other. Pour any excess marinade over the steaks and wrap the foil around the steaks. Leave to marinate in a refrigerator for at least 3 hours. Remove the steaks from the marinade and place on an oiled grill. Cook for about 6 minutes each side, spooning over any excess marinade as they cook. Serve garnished with the rosemary sprigs.

SERVES

4

FLUMMOXED VENISON

—————

900 g/2 lb venison, cubed

450 ml/¾ pint/2 cups mead
or red wine

2 bay leaves

1 bouquet garni

25 g/1 oz/¼ cup plain
(all-purpose) flour

50 g/2 oz/¼ cup butter

2 onions, chopped

2 carrots, chopped

150 ml/¼ pint/⅔ cup Irish stout

25 g/1 oz/¼ cup cornflour
(cornstarch)

¼ teaspoon salt

¼ teaspoon freshly ground
black pepper

Friaries and monasteries were traditionally self-sufficient in that they tended their own livestock and cultivated the land for food. Each also had its own fish pond to provide for the religious observance of eating only fish on Fridays. The monks and friars also made their own mead, country wine and ale. In the following recipe, the word 'flummoxed' means bewildered, an apt term for one who may have imbibed too much home-made mead!

Place the venison in a glass or ceramic bowl, pour over the mead or wine, add the bay leaves and bouquet garni, cover and leave to marinate overnight. Remove the meat from the marinade and pat dry on kitchen paper. Roll the meat in the flour, shaking off any excess. Heat the butter in a large saucepan and sauté the meat until browned on all sides. Strain the marinade over the meat and add the onions and carrots. Bring to the boil, then cover and simmer for about 1½ hours until tender. Blend the stout with the cornflour, stir into the saucepan and bring to the boil. Season with salt and pepper and simmer for 2 minutes, stirring until the sauce thickens, then serve hot.

CLASSIC BROWN SAUCE FOR MEAT OR VENISON

Many meat dishes are ideally accompanied by a brown sauce, often made with the gravy from the cooked meat instead of the stock in this recipe. This version, including port or red wine, is perfect for game. For other meats, you can omit this extra flavouring.

Heat the dripping and sauté the onion, carrot and bacon until brown. Stir in the flour and cook gently for 15 minutes. Slowly add the stock, stirring well until smooth. Add the port or wine and tomato purée, and season with salt and pepper. Bring to the boil and simmer for 30 minutes. Rub the sauce through a sieve before serving.

2 tablespoons beef dripping

1 onion, chopped

1 carrot, thinly sliced

2 bacon rashers (slices), rinded and chopped

25 g/1 oz/¼ cup plain (all-purpose) flour

450 ml/¾ pint/2 cups stock

2 tablespoons port or red wine

1 teaspoon tomato purée (paste)

¼ teaspoon salt

¼ teaspoon freshly ground black pepper

SERVES

4

BREAD SAUCE

300 ml/½ pint/1¼ cups milk
1 onion, quartered
1 bay leaf
50 g/2 oz/1 cup fresh white
breadcrumbs
1 tablespoon butter
1 tablespoon single (light) cream
salt and freshly ground black pepper

Another classic sauce, this can be served with game, meat or poultry dishes.

Place the milk in a saucepan with the onion and bay leaf and bring almost to the boil. Remove from the heat, cover and set aside for 30 minutes. Strain into a clean pan and stir in the breadcrumbs, butter and cream, then season to taste with salt and pepper.

Desserts and Drinks

Ireland's brewing industry has a long history going back to medieval times. During the 1200s, the waters of the Poddle River in Dublin provided the first of the raw materials for ale brewing, and local ale fast became the island's national drink. By the mid-1660s Dublin was the centre of the Irish ale business and there were more than 90 brew pubs and almost 2,000 ale houses in a city of only 4,000 families.

As early as 1670, Giles Mee was brewing an ordinary ale on a site near Dublin city's old entrance, St James's Gate. Then in about 1693, the brewing rights were transferred to Sir Mark Rainsford, and the business remained in that family until the brewery was leased to a John Paul Espinasse in 1715. On his death in 1750, the brewery went into disuse for a decade.

During the mid-eighteenth century in London, an ale made popular by the fruit and vegetable porters of Covent Garden, and those working in Billingsgate fish market, became known as porter. The addition of roasted barley to the ale gave the drink a distinctive dark colour

A little learning is a dang'rous thing; Drink deep, or taste not the Pierian spring; There shallow draughts intoxicate the brain, And drinking largely sobers us again.

Alexander Pope

and a slightly malty taste. In Dublin in 1759, a 34-year-old Irishman named Arthur Guinness decided that the English were not the only ones who could brew a fine porter, and approached the owner of the derelict St James's Brewery. With true Irish optimism, Guinness signed a 9,000-year lease on the brewery, agreeing to a £45-a-year rent. To see this lease out, Arthur Guinness would have to live until he was 9,034 years of age, beating Methuselah by 8,065 years! However, he began his business by first brewing a traditional Dublin ale, and later developing a strong porter which he called Extra Stout Porter, later shortened to stout, or Guinness stout. The popularity of his new brew overtook that of the local ale and it was soon being transported around Ireland through the newly constructed canal network. In 1803, Arthur Guinness passed away at the ripe old age of 78, handing the business over to his son, also named Arthur.

By the early part of the nineteenth century, the Guinness brewery was producing 66,000 barrels of stout a year, but the largest brewery was, in fact, Beamish and Crawford of Cork, which produced 100,000 barrels. By 1833, however, Guinness had become the largest brewery in Ireland and, by the time of Arthur Guinness II's death in 1855, had become the largest brewery in the world. The brewery was revamped in 1886 and even contained its own railway!

Guinness very quickly developed a strong export trade and even under the first Arthur Guinness, Guinness West Indies Porter was being shipped to the Caribbean. Guinness Strong Foreign Extra Stout (FES), with its 7.5 per cent alcohol content, was brewed in much the same way. This was developed by Arthur Guinness II especially for the export trade. The stout is matured for three months in wooden barrels, then blended with a young stout. So popular was the Guinness stout in England that a branch of the brewery was opened in Park Royal in London in 1936. Guinness went on to establish more breweries abroad, including Nigeria, Malaysia, Cameroon, Jamaica and Ghana. Guinness is now brewed in more than 45 different countries in all five continents and sold in 55 countries.

Guinness stout is made entirely with Irish products: 90,000 tons of home-grown barley are used each year, as are local hops, yeast and Ireland's famous water. The brewery stands near the banks of Dublin's River Liffey, although the water used for brewing comes from the Wicklow Mountains. Guinness begins as a sweet liquid known as 'wort', made by straining a 'mash' made from roasted and milled barley and water through a device known as a 'kieve'. Hops are added to the wort before it is boiled in huge coppers for one and a half hours, when the wort is left to settle for around 40 minutes, then left to cool. Yeast is then added to start the fermentation process, converting the nutrients and sugars in the wort into alcohol. An unfermented wort, known as 'gyle', is then added to the beer, which undergoes a second fermentation and is left to mature. The beer is clarified and, most importantly, tasted before distribution.

The final product itself, the celebrated Irish stout – known variously as the wine of the country, the icon of Irishness, the dark stuff, the parish priest or the blonde in the black skirt – is the ideal accompaniment to Ireland's traditional fare, especially cheese, meat dishes and seafood, which is why it is often called the essence of good living. The Guinness brewery not only produces the famous draught and bottled stout, however – it also produces beers, lager and cider. Cider is one of the first alcoholic beverages ever to be fermented. It is thought that the art of cider-making in Ireland originated with the advent of the Vikings, and the drink quickly became more popular than the local mead. Today's Irish cider can vary from two to eight per cent alcohol.

Whilst Guinness is the beer of 'Dublin's fair city', Cork also has two major breweries: Murphy's and Beamish. The country's second largest brewers, James J. Murphy was established at Lady's Well in Cork in 1856.

Murphy's began by brewing porter, but switched to stout as its popularity grew. Lane's Southgate Brewery was established in Cork in 1758, and was then taken over by Beamish and Crawford, which was initially the Cork Porter Brewery, founded in 1792. There are also several breweries in Ulster, including the Herald brewery at Lisburn and Hilden's brewery in Coleraine. A newcomer to the Irish stout scene is Caffrey's, and there are several other independent breweries, such as Smithwicks and Whitewater, which brew ales, stout and porter.

Nothing is wasted in the process of brewing stout, as all the by-products go back to the land. Farmers use as animal feed the 'screenings', or barley too small for brewing; the 'combings', or little roots grown by the partially germinated barley; the 'trub', the waste produced after yeast is added to the wort; and any surplus yeast.

One famous stout drink that is distinctly un-Irish is Black Velvet. Black Velvet is made with equal quantities of iced stout and champagne, poured into a glass simultaneously but not stirred, and drunk whilst the bubbles remain.

'There's more friendship in a glass of whiskey than in a barrel of buttermilk' is an old Irish saying, and as far back as the sixteenth century, Queen Elizabeth I once commented that Irish whiskey was her only true Irish

Here's brandy! Come, fill up your tumbler,
Or ale, if your liking be humbler,
And, while you've a shilling,
Keep filling and swilling,
A fig for the growls of the grumbler!

From the drinking song
by John O'Toumy (1708–75)

friend – although this may have had more to do with the politics of the day than her real opinion of the whiskey!

Irish whiskey has been distilled from a base of barley and malted barley in Ireland for centuries, and records of whiskey distilling date back to the sixth century. The whiskey is made with barley dried on a solid floor over fires, which prevents the smoke from permeating the barley. For Scotch whisky, on the other hand, the grain is dried over peat fires, imparting a different flavour to the grain. The Irish method ensures a smoothness which peat-fire heat cannot attain. Most Irish whiskey is pot stilled three times and matured for around five years before reaching the market.

The oldest commercial whiskey distillery in the world is Bushmills in Cork on the banks of the River Bush, and the company was licensed to distil whiskey in 1608. Other well-known distillers are Powers in Dublin, and the Jamieson label, with numerous ages and types of whiskey, from County Antrim. There is also the Paddy range of whiskies, and Redbreast, Green Spot and Tullamore Dew. Less well known are the whiskeys of the Cooley distillery on the Cooley peninsula near Dundalk in County Louth, in the east of Ireland, which are aged in the original Locke's Distillery in Kilbeggan, County Westmeath. These include Connemara, a single malt which has a local, peaty flavour similar to the blended Irish Inishowen; the Derry single malt known as Tyrconnell with its oily, woody flavour; the excellent light whiskey named Millar's after an old Dublin tipple; and Kilbeggan with its delightful aroma.

Drinking toasts is a common Irish custom, and in the early days, the peasant's drinking vessel was a wooden mug, or *madder*. However, in the grand country houses, some drinking glasses were long and thin without a base, so the drinker would have to drink the entire contents before replacing it on the table. More than a few toasts with this form of drinking glass would be unwise! As in every country in the world, the Irish have their form of 'Cheers': a toast is drunk with the word 'Slainte!' or 'good health'. One landlord famous for his toasts and drinking songs was John O'Toumy, who presided over a popular inn in Mungret Street, Limerick, in the 1700s. The inn served as a meeting place for poets and many a bard learned his art at O'Toumy's bar.

Most people have heard of the clandestine distilling of an alcoholic spirit in Ireland, known as poteen, or poitin, which means 'little pot still'. With possibly more names than the number of accounts of sightings of the little people, poteen is variously known as holy water, mountain dew, water of life, or a string of other euphemisms. Originally thought to date back to the sixth century, distilling poteen became widespread many years

O'Toumy! you boast yourself handy
At selling good ale and bright brandy,
But the fact is your liquor Makes every one sicker,
I tell you that, I, your friend Andy!

From Andrew MacGrath's
reply to O'Toumy's drinking song

On firm land only exercise your skill,
There you may play and safely drink your fill.

Epitaph to a drowned drunken fiddler

ago when the tax on whiskey became unacceptably high, and each distiller would create their own unique recipe, usually involving potatoes and grain. This home-brewed spirit has been illegal in Ireland since 1661, under King Charles II's laws, but today a commercially made poteen is available.

In one of the traditional recipes, the *usquebagh* begins as a wash of grapes, raisins, black treacle, sugar and yeast in water, which is left to ferment for three weeks. The wash is strained into a boiler, in which it is heated to boiling point and begins to give off steam. The steam is channelled into a long, spiral, copper pipe, known as the worm, which runs down into a barrel filled with cold water. When the hot steam cools, it condenses in the tube and can be tapped off as a clear, 140-degree-proof poteen – much too powerful to drink! After the first quantity has been bled off, the tipple becomes weaker and more palatable. The run, as it is called, takes around three hours from boiling to bottling. The poteen is then tested for strength and taste. Its alcoholic purity is tested by dipping a twist of paper in the brew, then lighting it. The blue flame should not consume the paper. A finger is subjected to the same treatment and the tester should remain unscathed by the ordeal. The third, and best, test is to sample the poteen by drinking it!

TIPSY PUDDING

Preheat the oven to 200°C/400°F/gas mark 6 and line a wide, flat baking sheet with oiled baking foil. Whisk together the sugar and eggs in a bowl over a pan of hot water until pale. Fold in the flour and vanilla essence, then pour the batter into the baking sheet. Bake in the oven for about 8 minutes until springy to the touch. Turn out on to a cornflour-dusted surface and remove the foil. Spread the jam over the surface of the cake and roll up from the long side. Set on dish to cool, then pour the whiskey and sherry over the top.

To make the topping, whisk the egg yolks, cornflour, sugar and vanilla essence into the milk in a bowl set over a pan of simmering water. Stir over a low heat until the mixture is thick, then pour over the roll, leave to cool and refrigerate for 1 hour. Whip the cream until stiff, then spread over pudding and decorate with toasted almonds.

For the pudding

75 g/3 oz/⅓ cup caster (superfine) sugar

3 eggs

75 g/3 oz/¾ cup plain (all-purpose) flour

½ teaspoon vanilla essence (extract)

2 tablespoons cornflour (cornstarch)

225 g/8 oz/⅔ cup fruit jam (conserve)

120 ml/4 fl oz/½ cup Irish whiskey

5 tablespoons sherry

For the topping

2 egg yolks

1 teaspoon cornflour (cornstarch)

1 tablespoon granulated sugar

¼ teaspoon vanilla essence (extract)

300 ml/½ pint/1¼ cups milk

300 ml/½ pint/1¼ cups double (heavy) cream

50 g/2 oz/½ cup almonds, toasted

ORCHARD APPLES
IN WHISKEY SAUCE

SERVES

4

4 red eating (dessert) apples

4 green eating (dessert) apples

50 g/2 oz/¼ cup butter

1 cinnamon stick

10 cloves

50 g/2 oz/¼ cup caster
(superfine) sugar

4 teaspoons clear honey

For the sauce

6 egg yolks

75 g/3 oz/⅓ cup caster
(superfine) sugar

6 tablespoons Irish whiskey

Poach the red apples in a saucepan of simmering water for 6 minutes. Remove and leave to cool. Make the sauce by whisking the egg yolks, sugar and whiskey in a bowl set over a pan of simmering water until pale and thick. (Do not overheat or the sauce will curdle.) Remove from the heat and keep warm. Slice off and keep the tops of the red apples, then carefully scoop out and chop the flesh. Discard the core. Peel, quarter and core the green apples and cut into segments. Melt the butter and sauté the apple segments with the cinnamon, cloves, sugar and honey until the apples are cooked. Discard the spices and simmer to reduce the remaining liquid. Arrange the red apple flesh in the bottom of their hollowed-out skins and arrange the segments on top. Place the apples in the centre of warm plates, then pour the sauce from the pan around the edges. Spoon the whiskey sauce over the top of the apples, replace the tops and serve.

CARRAGHEEN COCOA DESSERT

SERVES
4

Soak the carragheen in cold water for 2 hours, then drain. Bring milk and water to the boil, then add the carragheen and simmer for 1 hour. Purée in a food processor or blender. Mix the cocoa, sugar and vanilla essence with a little milk, add this paste to the carragheen mixture and stir well. Chill, then serve with the whipped cream.

2 large handfuls of dried carragheen

900 ml/1½ pints/3¾ cups milk

300 ml/½ pint/1¼ cups water

4 tablespoons cocoa (unsweetened chocolate) powder

3 tablespoons caster (superfine) sugar

2 drops of vanilla essence (extract)

300 ml/½ pint/1¼ cups double (heavy) cream, whipped

179

YALLER SPOTTED DOG

SERVES
4

225 g/8 oz/2 cups plain
(all-purpose) flour

225 g/8 oz/2 cups corn meal

1 teaspoon caster (superfine) sugar

1 teaspoon salt

1 teaspoon bicarbonate of soda
(baking soda)

5 tablespoons buttermilk

100 g/4 oz/⅔ cup sultanas
(golden raisins)

1 tablespoon milk

Preheat the oven to 180°C/350°F/gas mark 4. Sift the flour, corn meal, sugar, salt and bicarbonate of soda into a bowl, then stir in the buttermilk until the mixture becomes tacky. Turn out on to a floured board and knead in the sultanas. Shape into a round, flat cake, cut a cross on the top and brush with the milk. Bake in the oven for about 45 minutes until the cake sounds hollow when tapped on the base. Serve warm with lots of butter.

STOUT CISTE

Preheat the oven to 160°C/325°F/gas mark 3. Place the stout, sugar and butter in a pan over a low heat and stir until the butter melts. Mix in the fruit, bring to the boil and simmer for 4 minutes. Remove from the heat and leave to cool. Mix the flour, allspice and soda in a bowl, then stir in the fruit mixture and the eggs. Turn into a greased and lined 20 cm (8 inch) cake tin. Bake in the oven for 2 hours until a knife inserted in the centre comes out clean. Leave to cool in the tin before turning out.

300 ml/½ pint/1¼ cups stout

225 g/8 oz/1 cup soft brown sugar

225 g/8 oz/1 cup butter

225 g/8 oz/1⅓ cups raisins

225 g/8 oz/1⅓ cups sultanas
(golden raisins)

225 g/8 oz/1⅓ cups currants

50 g/2 oz/¼ cup glacé (candied)
cherries, quartered

550 g/1¼ lb/5 cups plain
(all-purpose) flour

1 teaspoon ground allspice

½ teaspoon bicarbonate of soda
(baking soda)

3 eggs, beaten

SERVES
4

SWEET HONEYED OATS

300 ml/½ pint/1¼ cups milk
175 g/6 oz/1½ cups rolled oats
50 g/2 oz/¼ cup caster
(superfine) sugar
2 tablespoons Irish heather honey
25 g/1 oz/2 tablespoons butter
½ teaspoon ground cinnamon
½ teaspoon allspice
finely grated rind of 1 orange
3 eggs, separated

Bring the milk to the boil in a saucepan. Sprinkle in the oats and simmer gently for 5 minutes, stirring. Beat in the sugar, honey, butter, spices and orange rind. Remove from the heat and leave to cool slightly, then beat in the egg yolks. Whisk the egg whites until stiff, then carefully fold them into the mixture. Turn into a greased pudding basin, cover with pleated greaseproof paper and place in a large saucepan. Fill the saucepan with boiling water to come half way up the sides of the basin, cover and steam for 2 hours, topping up with boiling water as necessary. Turn on to a dish and serve with fragrant honey and cream.

CRANACHAN

Whip the cream until stiff, then fold in the honey and whiskey. Stir in the rolled oats and almonds, then the lemon juice. Chill, then serve garnished with orange slices.

350 ml/12 fl oz/1⅓ cups double (heavy) cream

4 tablespoons clear honey

4 tablespoons Irish whiskey

75 g/3 oz/¾ cup rolled oats, toasted

50 g/2 oz/½ cup ground almonds, toasted

1 teaspoon lemon juice

1 orange, sliced

HEATHER HONEY MOUSSE

SERVES
4

4 large eggs, separated
450 g/1 lb/1⅓ cups clear
heather honey

Mix the egg yolks with the honey in a bowl set over a pan of gently simmering water. Keep stirring until the mixture forms a custard. Remove the pan from the heat and leave to cool. Whisk the egg whites until they stand up in peaks, then gently fold into the cool mixture. Spoon into individual dishes and chill for 3–4 hours before serving.

BROSE

———

Although there are many variations, brose consists of a mixture of oatmeal, cream, honey and Irish whiskey. The Gaelic atholl, or atholl brose, is claimed by the Scots, but brose is originally thought to come from Ireland. Traditionally held to be a remedy for the common cold, the name of brose may have derived from the word 'ambrosia' or 'food of the gods'. Other experts suggest that the name stems from the word broth, and in Ireland to be called a 'broth of a fellow' is a compliment, as it means a 'really fine chap'.

Soak the oats in boiling water for 1 hour, then pour into a sieve. Press with the back of a spoon until most of the water is expelled. Whip the cream until stiff, then fold in the honey and whiskey. Stir in the oats and serve.

3 tablespoons rolled oats

300 ml/½ pint/1¼ cups double (heavy) cream

1 tablespoon clear honey

2 tablespoons Irish whiskey

RUSTIC RHUBARB TART

SERVES

4

350 g/12 oz puff pastry
450 g/1 lb rhubarb, sliced
175 g/6 oz/¾ cup butter, melted
175 g/6 oz/¾ cup soft brown sugar
**300 ml/½ pint/1¼ cups double
(heavy) cream**
**100 g/4 oz/½ cup caster
(superfine) sugar**
2 teaspoons Irish whiskey
4 sprigs of fresh mint

Preheat oven to 180°C/350°F/gas mark 4. Roll out the pastry on a lightly floured board, cut into four equal circles and turn up the edges of each one to make tart cases and place on a greased baking sheet. Divide the rhubarb equally between the tarts, then brush with the melted butter and sprinkle with the brown sugar. Cook in the oven for 30 minutes until the rhubarb is tender and the sugar has caramelized on top. Make the sauce by whipping the cream until stiff, then whisking in the caster sugar and whiskey. Serve the tarts with the whiskey cream and garnish with the sprigs of mint.

BRUIDEN TART

Preheat oven to 180°C/350°F/gas mark 4. Roll out the pastry on a lightly floured board and use to line four greased pie tins. Sprinkle the ground almonds over the pastry cases, place the apple slices on top and sprinkle with granulated sugar. Beat the egg yolks and caster sugar until pale and fluffy. Warm the cream slightly, then stir it into the egg and sugar mixture. Stir in the whiskey. Spoon a little of the cream mixture into each tart to cover the apples and reserve the remaining cream. Bake the tarts in the oven for 25–35 minutes until golden on top. Meanwhile, heat the remaining cream in a bowl set over a pan of gently simmering water and stir until it thickens, then serve with the tarts.

225 g/8 oz shortcrust pastry

50 g/2 oz/½ cup ground almonds

4 large cooking (tart) apples, peeled, cored and sliced

2 tablespoons granulated sugar

3 egg yolks, beaten

50 g/2 oz/¼ cup caster (superfine) sugar

300 ml/½ pint/1¼ cups double (heavy) cream

2 teaspoons Irish whiskey

MAKES
one 20 cm (8 inch) cake

2 eggs

75 g/3 oz/⅓ cup caster (superfine) sugar

50 g/2 oz/¼ cup butter

100 g/4 oz plain (semi-sweet) chocolate

50 g/2 oz/½ cup crushed hazelnuts

250 ml/8 fl oz/1 cup Irish whiskey

225 g/8 oz digestive biscuits (Graham crackers), crushed

3 tablespoons double (heavy) cream

50 g/2 oz/½ cup whole hazelnuts

50 g/2 oz/¼ cup glacé (candied) cherries

WHISKEY CHOCOLATE CAKE

Whisk together the eggs and sugar until pale. Melt the butter and chocolate in a pan, then fold in the egg mixture. Stir in the crushed hazelnuts and half the whiskey. Sprinkle the crushed biscuits into a greased and lined 20 cm (8 inch) cake tin. Pour the chocolate mixture into the tin and place in a refrigerator overnight. Whip the cream until stiff, then fold in the remaining whiskey. Turn out the cake, pipe the cream on the top and decorate with whole hazelnuts and glacé cherries.

AISLING APPLE CAKE

Preheat the oven to 200°C/400°F/gas mark 6. Rub the butter into the flour and baking powder. Stir in the sugar, then add the egg and enough of the milk to make a dough. Roll out half the dough and use to line a greased pie dish. Arrange the apples on the pastry, sprinkle with brown sugar and add the cloves. Roll out the remaining dough, cover the pie and seal the edges with a little milk. Cook in the oven for 40 minutes until browned.

100 g/4 oz/½ cup butter

225 g/8 oz/2 cups plain (all-purpose) flour

½ teaspoon baking powder

100 g/4 oz/½ cup granulated sugar

1 egg, lightly beaten

3 tablespoons milk

2 cooking (tart) apples, peeled, cored and chopped

2 tablespoons soft brown sugar

3 cloves

MACHA'S COFFEE MERINGUE

MAKES
one 20 cm (8 inch) cake

3 egg whites

75 g/3 oz/⅓ cup caster
(superfine) sugar

75 g/3 oz/½ cup icing
(confectioners') sugar

1½ tablespoons instant coffee

450 ml/¾ pint/2 cups double
(heavy) cream

2 tablespoons Irish whiskey

Preheat the oven to 120°C/250°F/gas mark 1. Whisk egg whites until stiff. Beat in the caster sugar. Sift the icing sugar and mix it with the coffee, then fold into the egg mixture. Spread the mixture into two 20 cm (8 inch) circles on a lined baking sheet and cook in the oven for 4 hours until hard and dry on the outside, but soft inside. Whip the cream until stiff, then stir in the whiskey. Spread the cream on the flat side of one meringue round and place the second meringue on top.

JAMIESON'S CAKE

———

Soak the fruit in the whiskey overnight. Preheat the oven to 160°C/325°F/gas mark 3. Cream the butter and soft brown sugar together until pale, then gradually add the beaten eggs and vanilla essence. Fold in the flour, baking powder and spices. Add the fruit and whiskey, orange rind and ground almonds. Spoon into a greased and lined 20 cm (8 inch) cake tin, sprinkle with the demerara sugar and bake in the oven for 1½ hours. Allow to cool in the tin.

350 g/12 oz/2 cups mixed dried fruit

75 g/3 oz/⅓ cup glacé (candied) cherries

120 ml/4 fl oz/½ cup Jamieson's or other Irish whiskey

175 g/6 oz/⅔ cup butter

175 g/6 oz/⅔ cup soft brown sugar

4 eggs, beaten

a few drops of vanilla essence (extract)

300 g/9 oz/2¼ cups plain (all-purpose) flour

2 teaspoons baking powder

2 teaspoons ground allspice

½ teaspoon cinnamon

finely grated rind of 1½ oranges

75 g/3 oz/¾ cup ground almonds

2 tablespoons demerara sugar

YELLOW MAN

SERVES

4

25 g/1 oz/2 tablespoons butter
450 g/1 lb/1⅓ cups golden
(light corn) syrup
225 g/8 oz/1 cup soft brown sugar
2 drops of rose essence (extract)
2 tablespoons white vinegar
1 teaspoon baking powder

Coat the inside of a saucepan with the melted butter. Pour in the syrup, sugar and rose essence, then the vinegar. Bring to the boil, then reduce to a simmer. With a wooden spoon, drop a little of the mixture into cold water. If it sets in the water, stir in the baking powder. When the mixture foams, pour it into a greased baking dish and leave to cool enough to handle. Pull the toffee-like mix until it turns yellow, then leave to set and break it into small pieces with a hammer.

Did you treat your
Mary-Ann
To dulse and yelloe man
At the ould Lammas Fair
in Ballycastle?

Early Irish children's rhyme

STOUT BERRY

———

Using the best of Irish ingredients – rolled oats and stout – this is said to be an excellent remedy for colds.

Heat the stout in a saucepan and stir in the oats, ginger and nutmeg. Bring to the boil, then simmer for 20 minutes. Strain into a warm jug, stir in the sugar, honey and lemon juice and serve very hot.

1.2 litres/2 pints/5 cups Irish stout

2 tablespoons rolled oats

1 teaspoon fresh finely chopped root ginger

½ teaspoon freshly grated nutmeg

2 tablespoons soft brown sugar

1 tablespoon honey

juice of ½ lemon

IRISH COFFEE

SERVES

1

2 tablespoons Irish whiskey
2 teaspoons soft brown sugar
fresh strong coffee
fresh double (heavy) cream

Warm a coffee cup or heat-resistant glass with hot water. Pour in the whiskey, then add sugar. Pour in the coffee, leaving a 3 cm (1¼ inch) space at the top. Top up with cream poured over the back of a teaspoon.

*Coffee (which makes
the politician wise,
And see thro' all things
with his half-shut eyes).*

Alexander Pope (1688–1744)

SCAILTIN

Also known as a Hot Irish, this classic dish would ideally finish off a meal of crubeens, or pigs' trotters, especially at a craic, or family celebration with local dance, song and convivial conversation. One important guest at these gatherings is a seanachai, or travelling storyteller, the modern equivalent of the ancient bards, or filis. In the early days, this concoction might have been served at the many local shebeens, or small taverns which sold illicit whiskey. It would be drunk from a madder, a wooden drinking cup, the name of which comes from meadar, from which mead was originally drunk.

Warm a glass with very hot water, then fill two-thirds full with boiling water. Dissolve the sugar in the water, then add the whiskey. Add the lemon slice, cloves, nutmeg and cinnamon, stirring gently. Hold in the hand, savour the aroma, sip slowly. Now order another!

1 teaspoon demerara sugar

1 extra large measure
of Irish whiskey

1 slice of lemon

6 cloves

a pinch of freshly grated nutmeg

a pinch of ground cinnamon

Give me chastity and continency — but not yet!

St Augustine

195

Glossary

UK	US
bacon rasher	bacon slice
baking foil	aluminum foil
baking sheet	cookie sheet
bicarbonate of soda	baking soda
biscuit cutter	cookie cutter
biscuits	cookies
black treacle	molasses
cake tin	cake pan
caster sugar	superfine sugar
casserole dish	dutch oven
celery sticks	celery stalks
chicory leaves	belgian endive
cocoa powder	unsweetened chocolate powder
cooking apples	tart apples
cornflour	cornstarch
courgette	zucchini
digestive biscuits	graham crackers
dill	dillweed
double cream	heavy cream
eating apple	dessert apple

UK	US
flaked almonds	slivered almonds
frying pan	skillet
glacé cherries	candied cherries
golden syrup	light corn syrup
greaseproof paper	waxed paper
grill	broiler
grilled	broiled
hard-boiled eggs	hard-cooked eggs
haricot beans	navy beans
icing sugar	confectioners' sugar
jam	conserve
ketchup	catsup
kitchen paper	paper towels
loaf tin	(loaf) pan
minced	ground
mixed peel	candied peel
pastry cutter	cookie cutter
pepper (red or green)	bell pepper
plain chocolate	semi-sweet chocolate
plain flour	all-purpose flour
prawns (normal)	shrimp
prawns (Dublin Bay)	saltwater crayfish
pudding basin	pudding mold
ramekin dishes	custard cups

UK	US
roasting tin	roasting pan
rose essence	rose extract
self-raising flour	self-rising flour
sieve	strainer
single cream	light cream
spring onions	scallions
sultanas	golden raisins
swiss roll	jelly roll
tomato purée	tomato paste
unsalted butter	sweet butter
vanilla essence	vanilla extract
vanilla pod	vanilla bean
wholemeal	wholewheat

Index